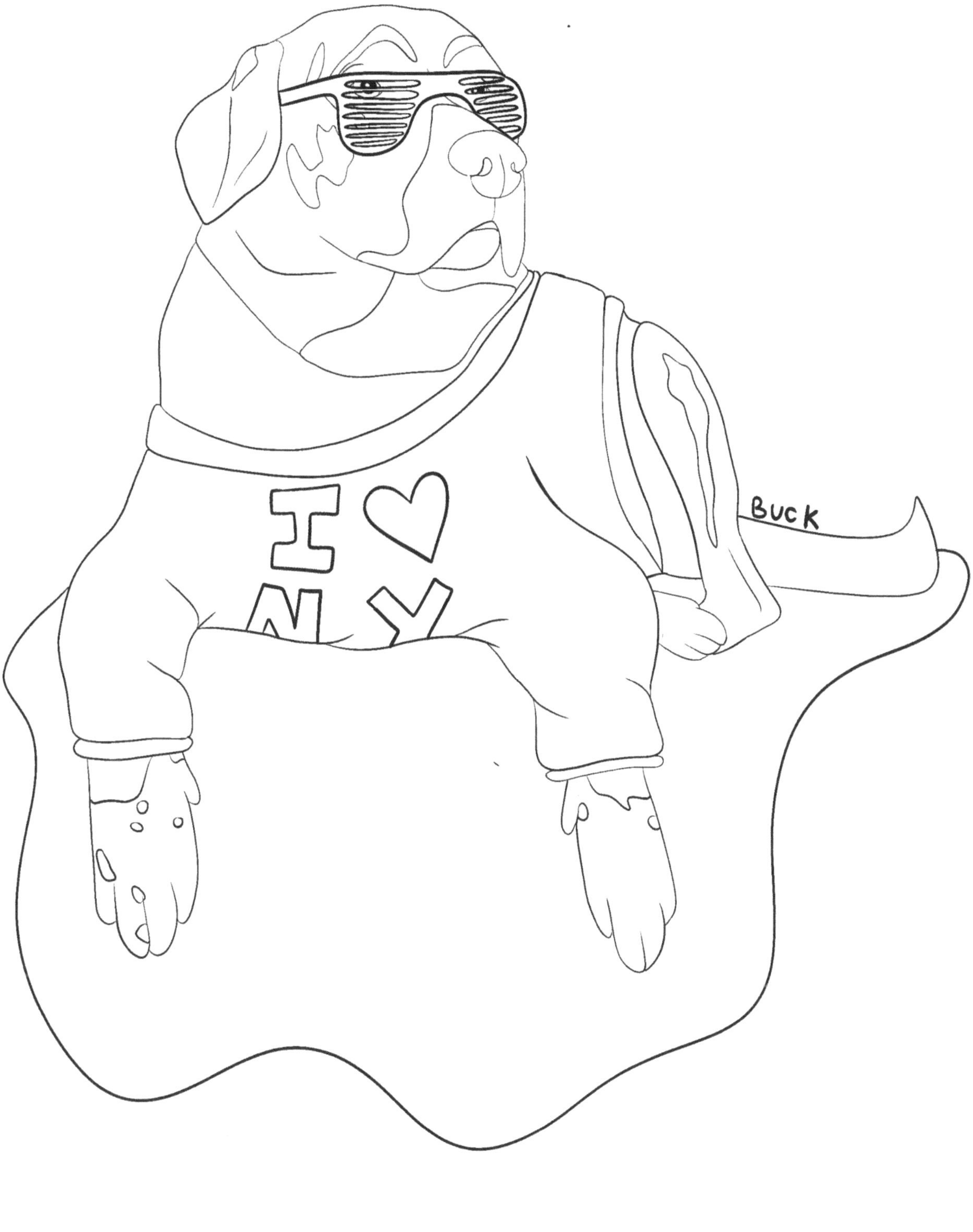
I ♥ NY
BUCK

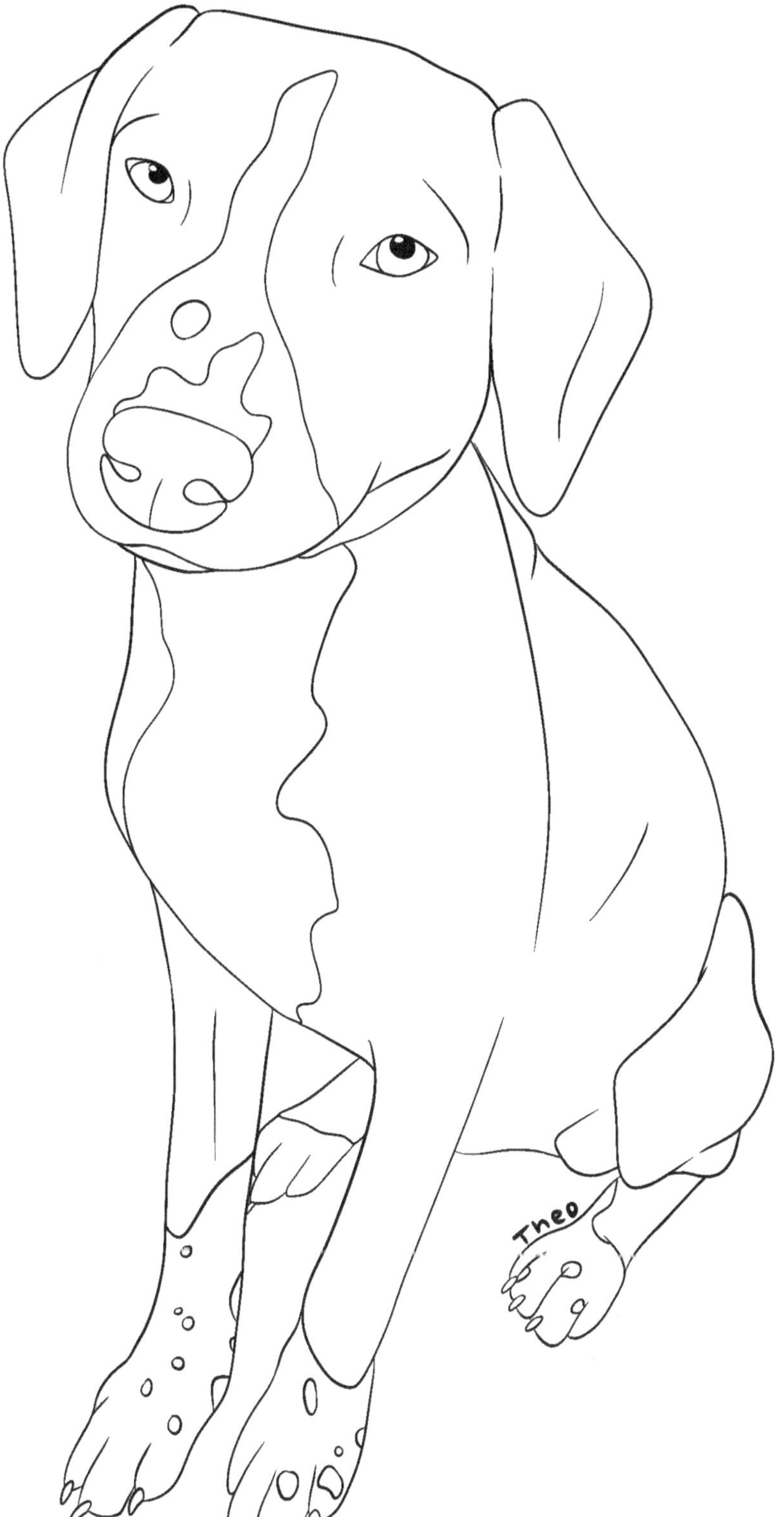
Theo

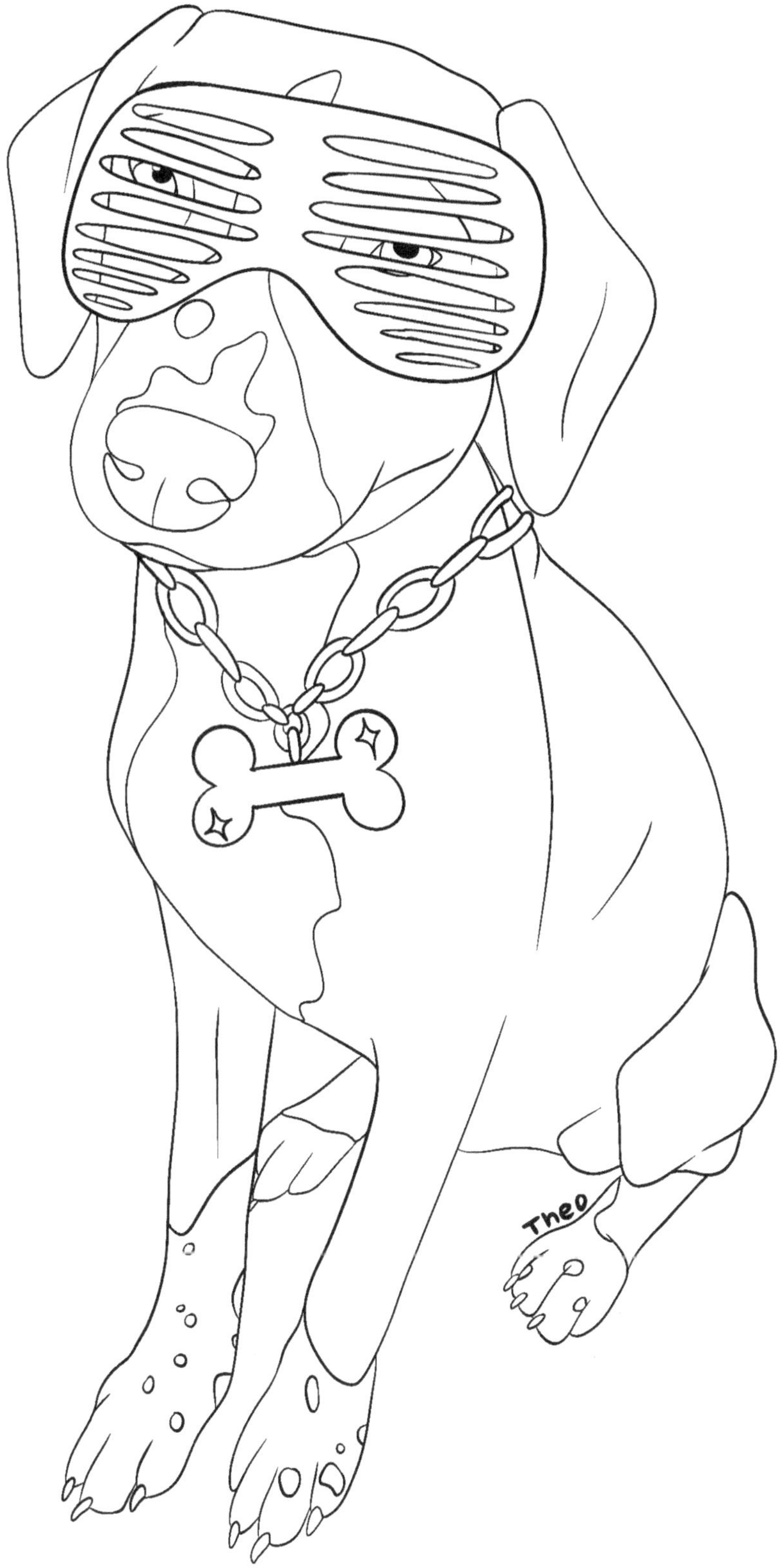
Theo

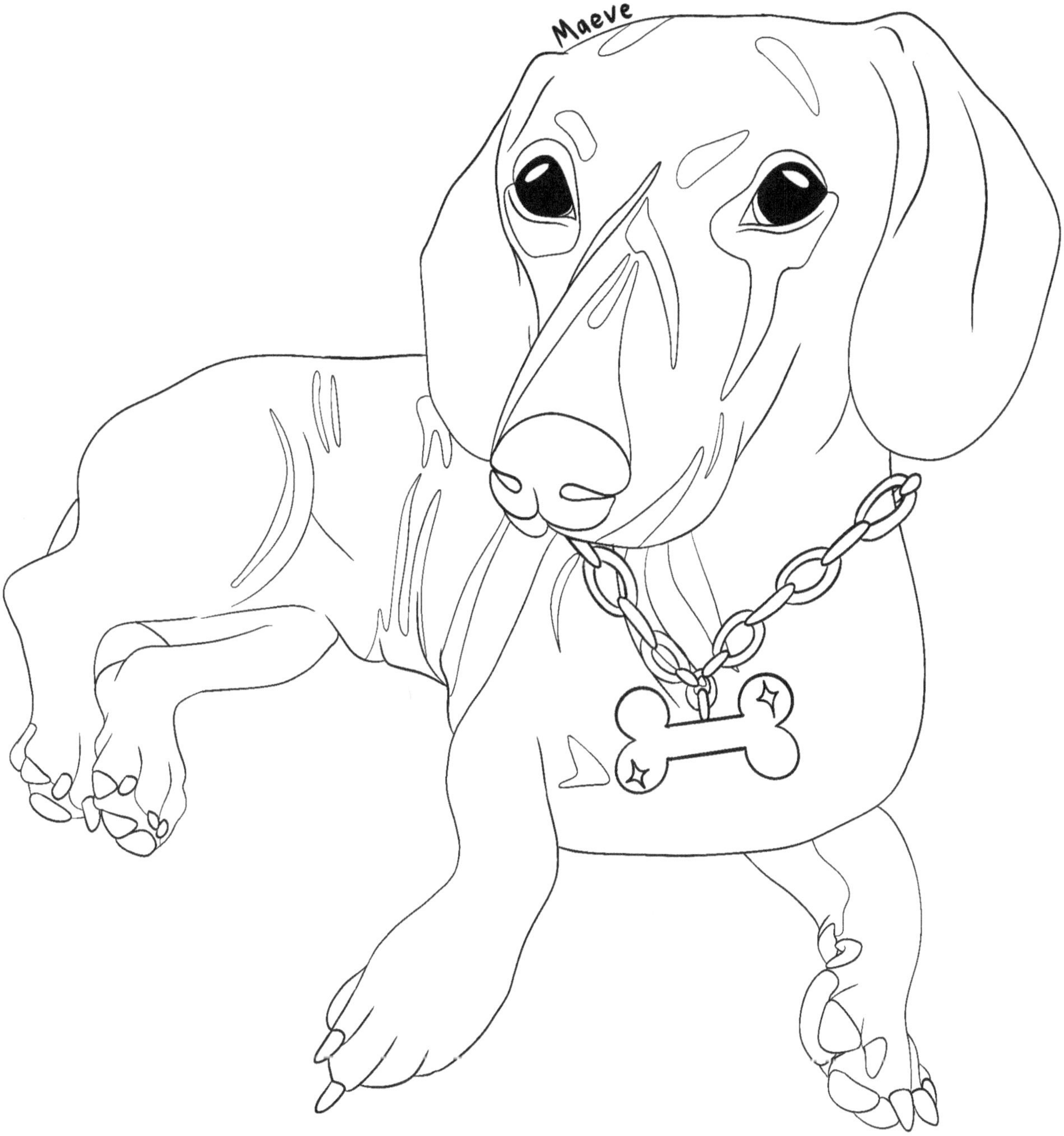
Maeve

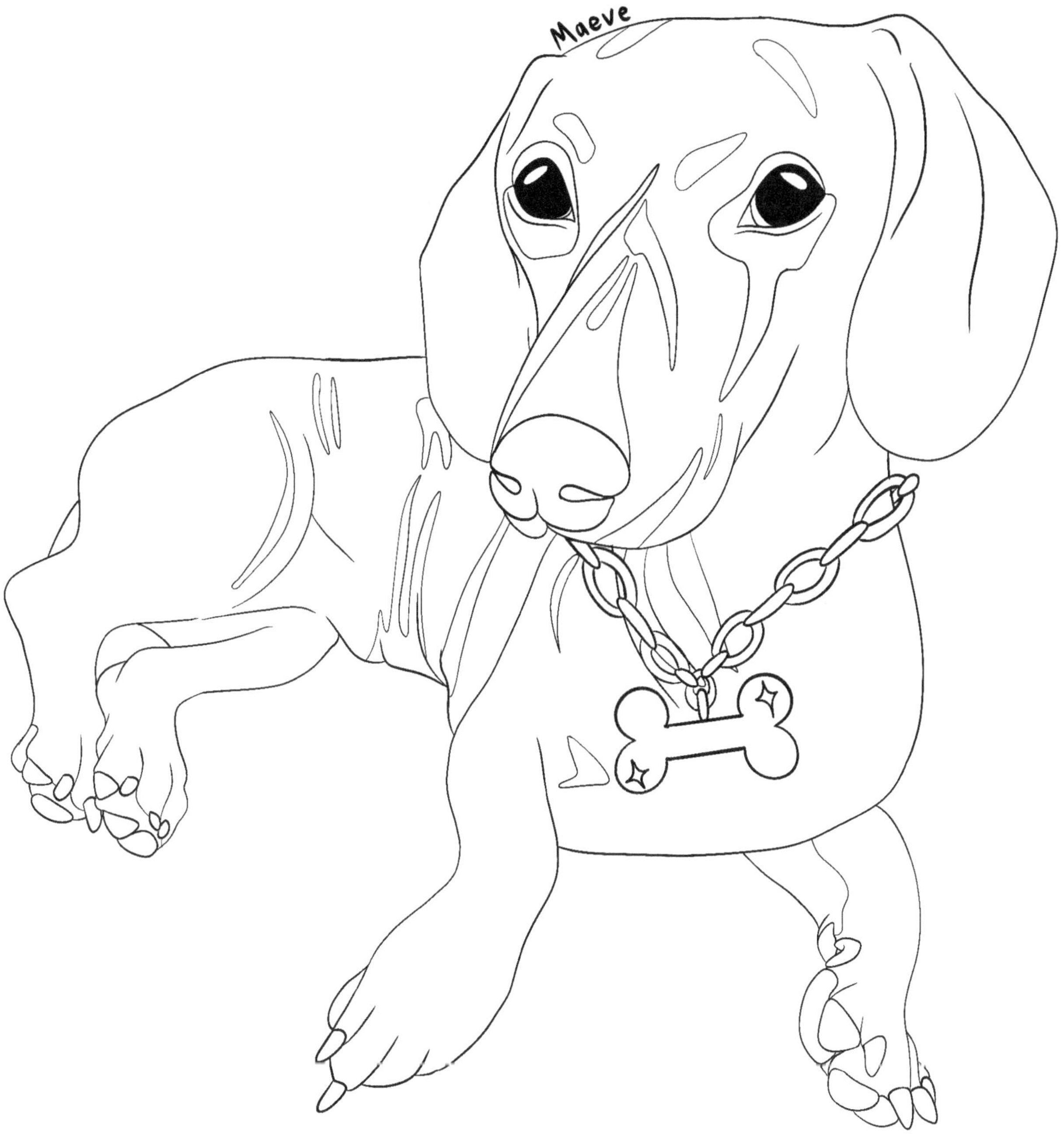
Maeve

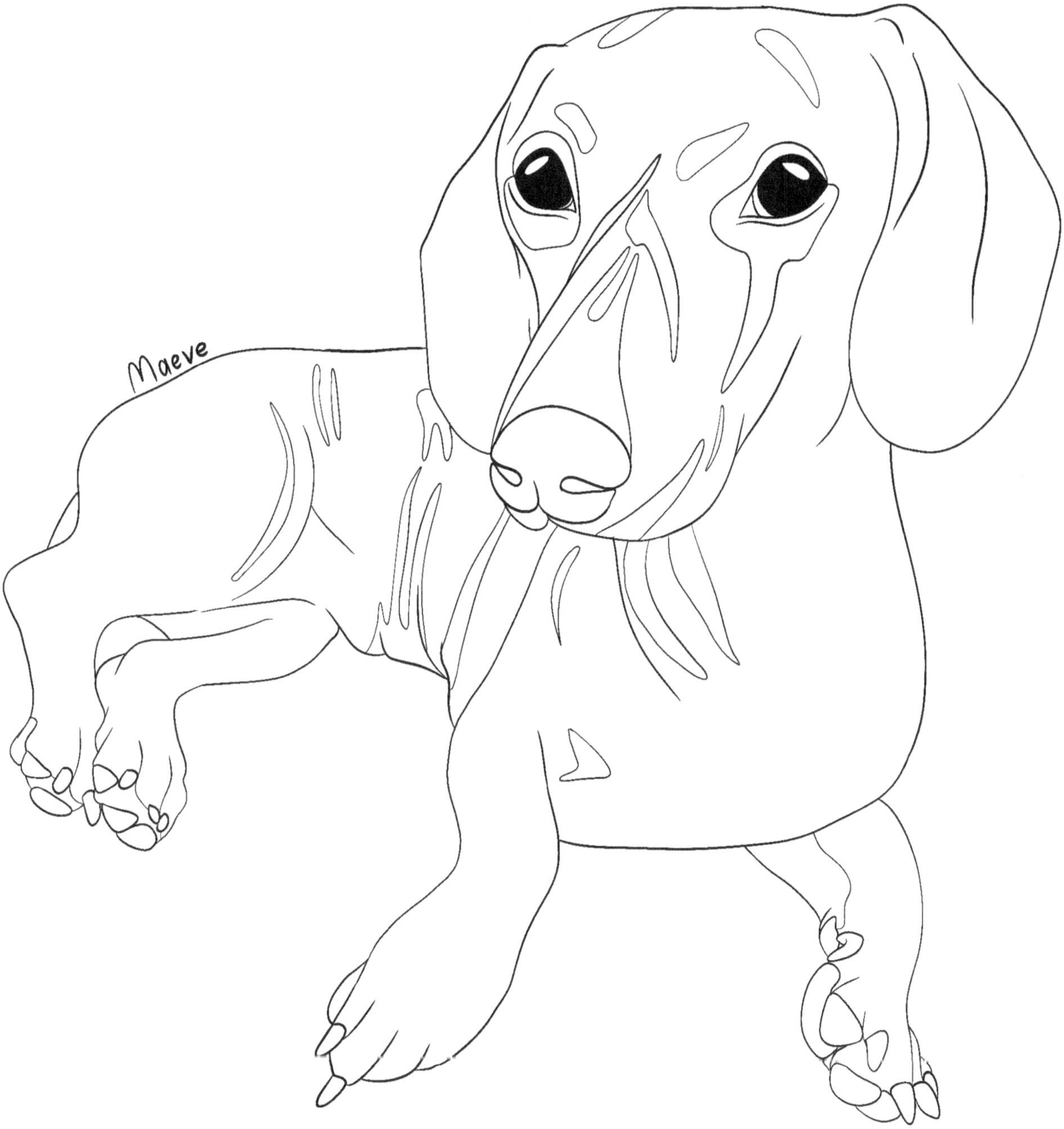
Maeve

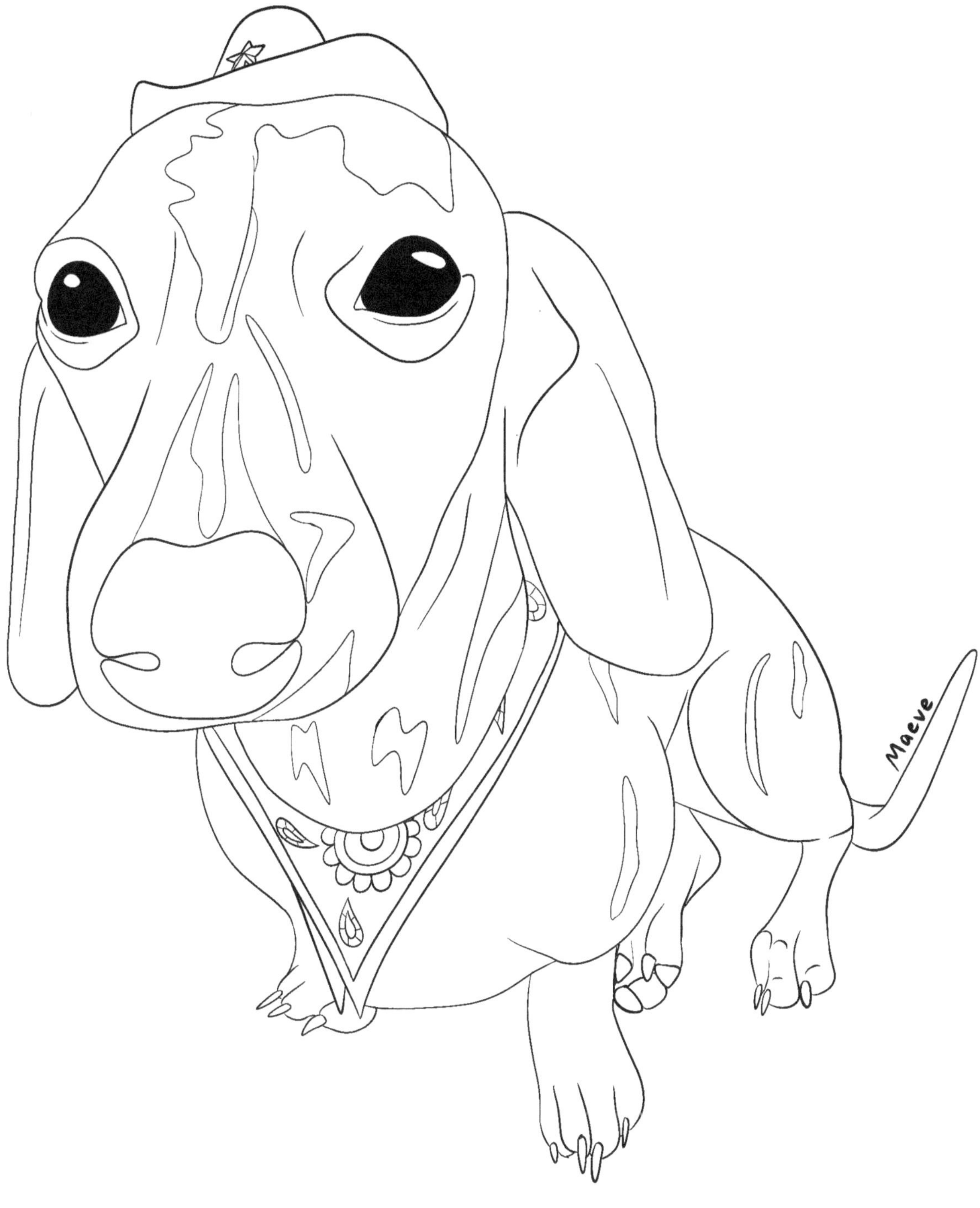
Maeve

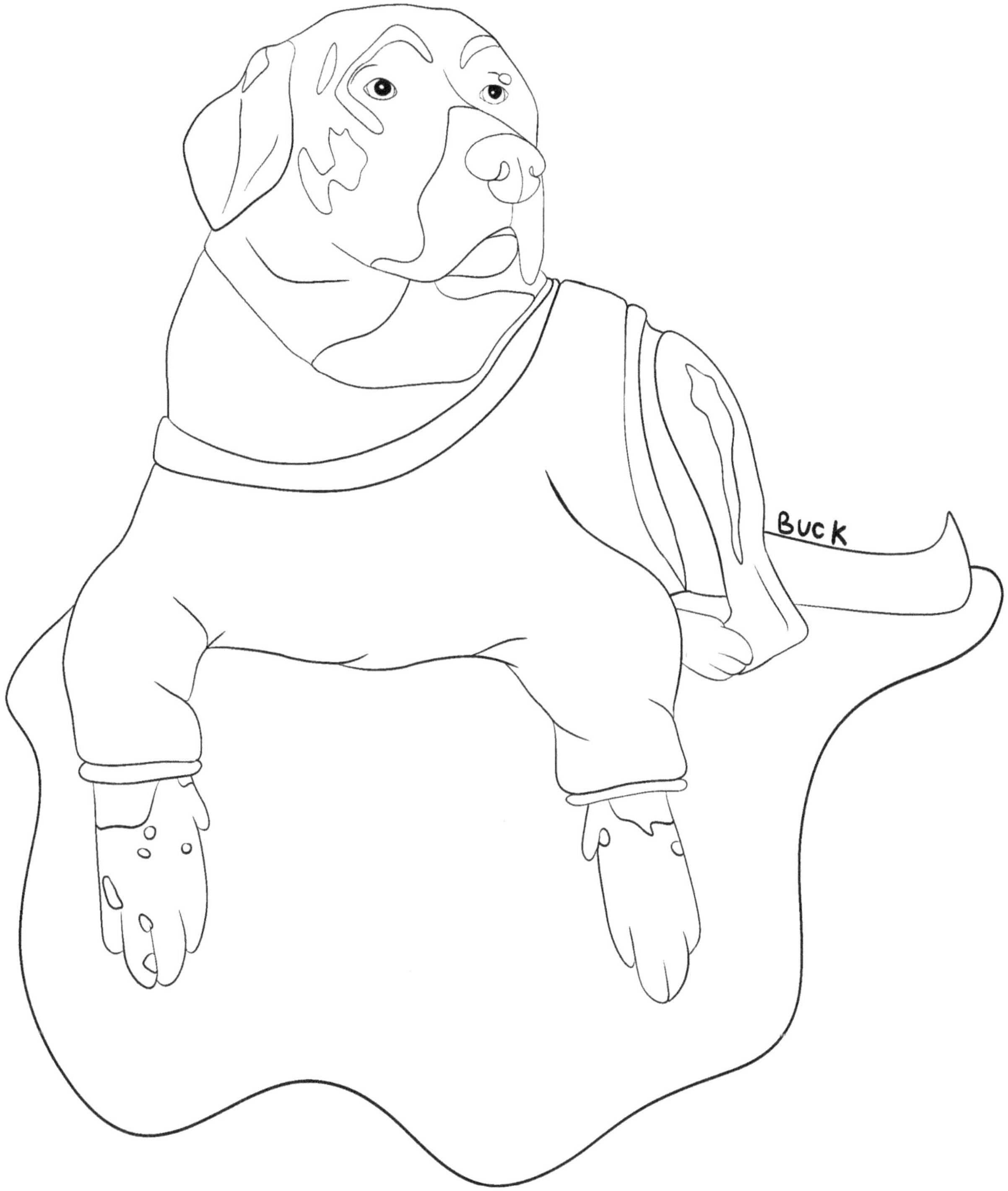
BUCK

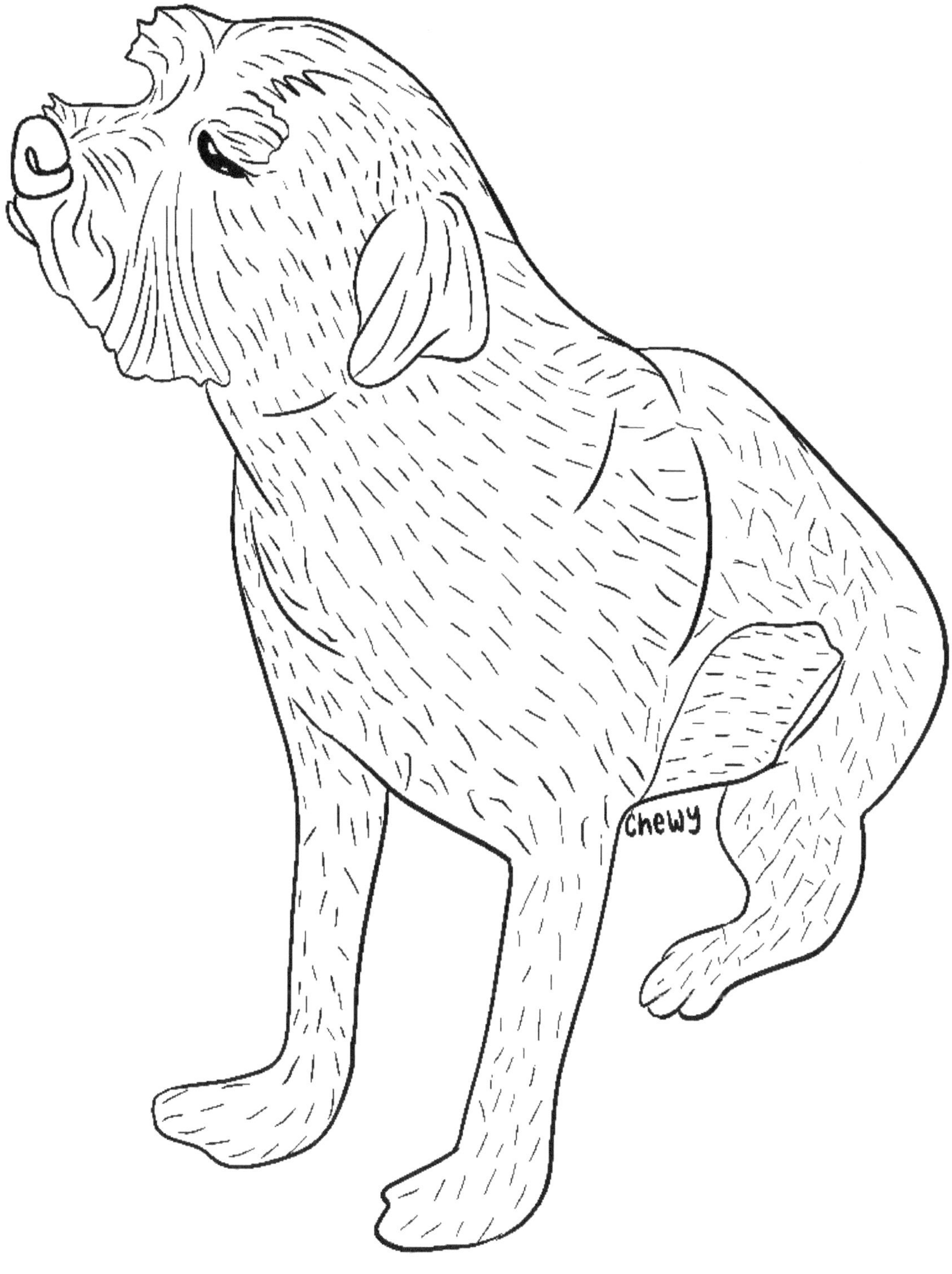
Chewy

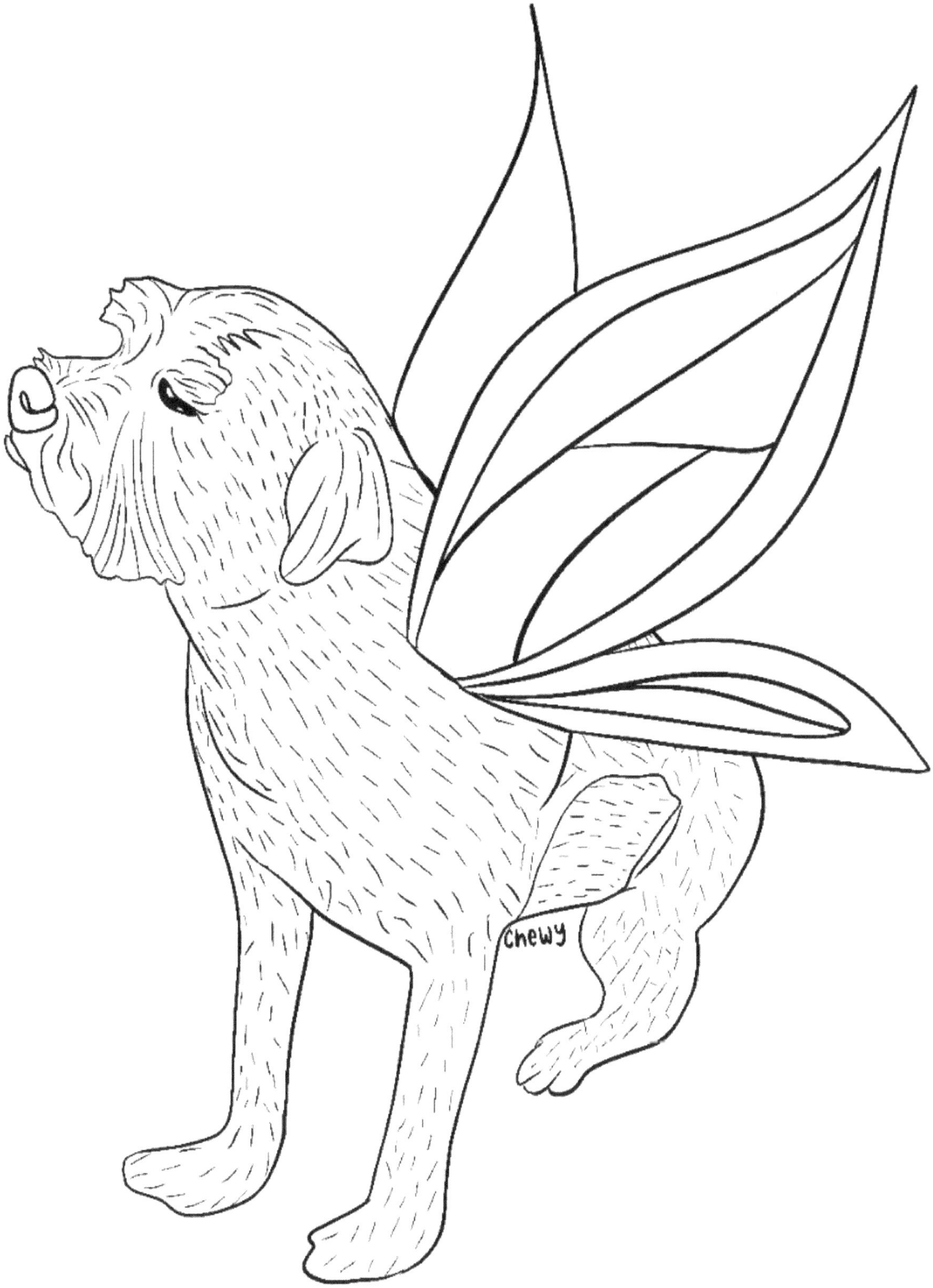
Chewy

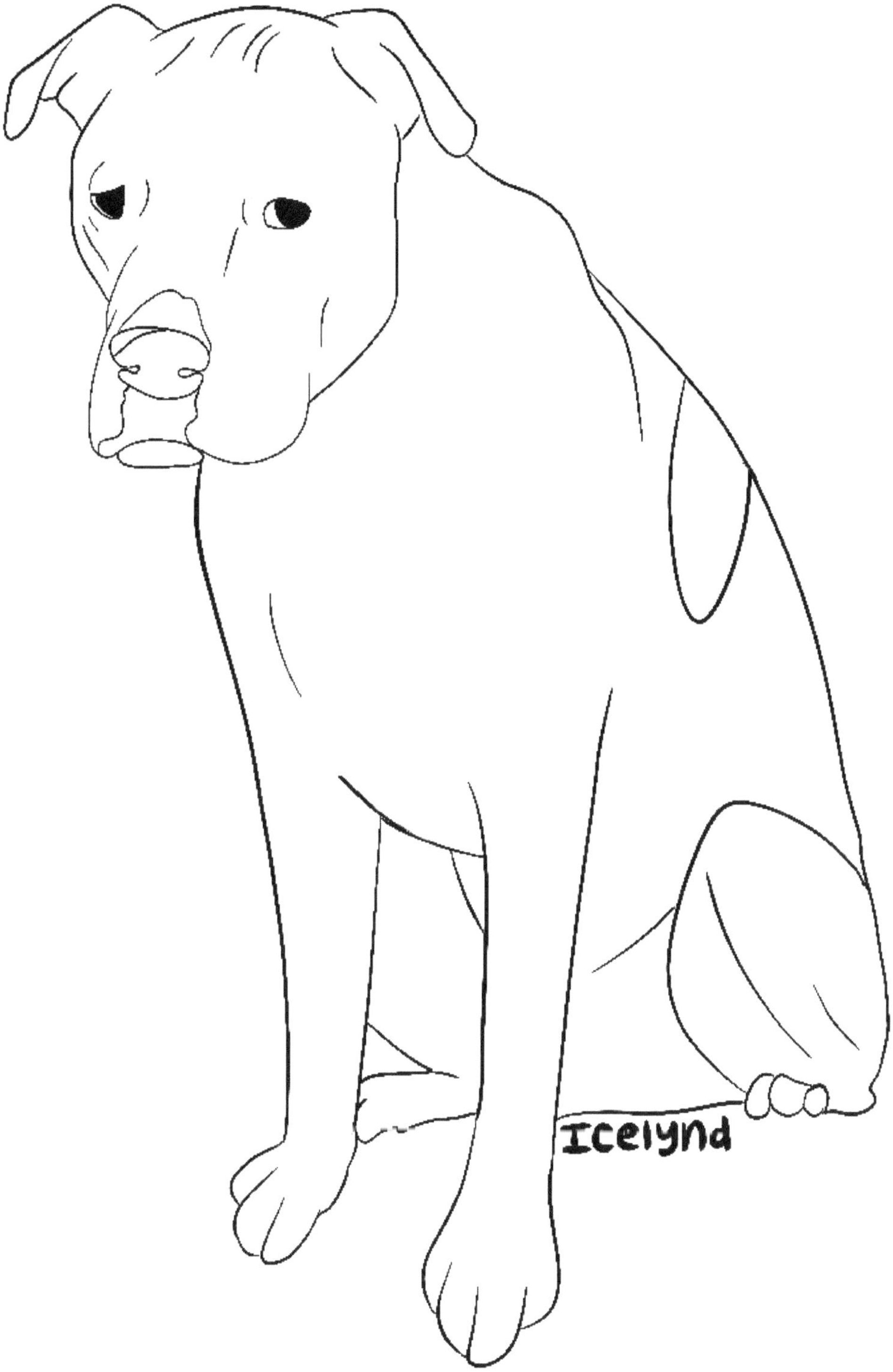
Icelynd

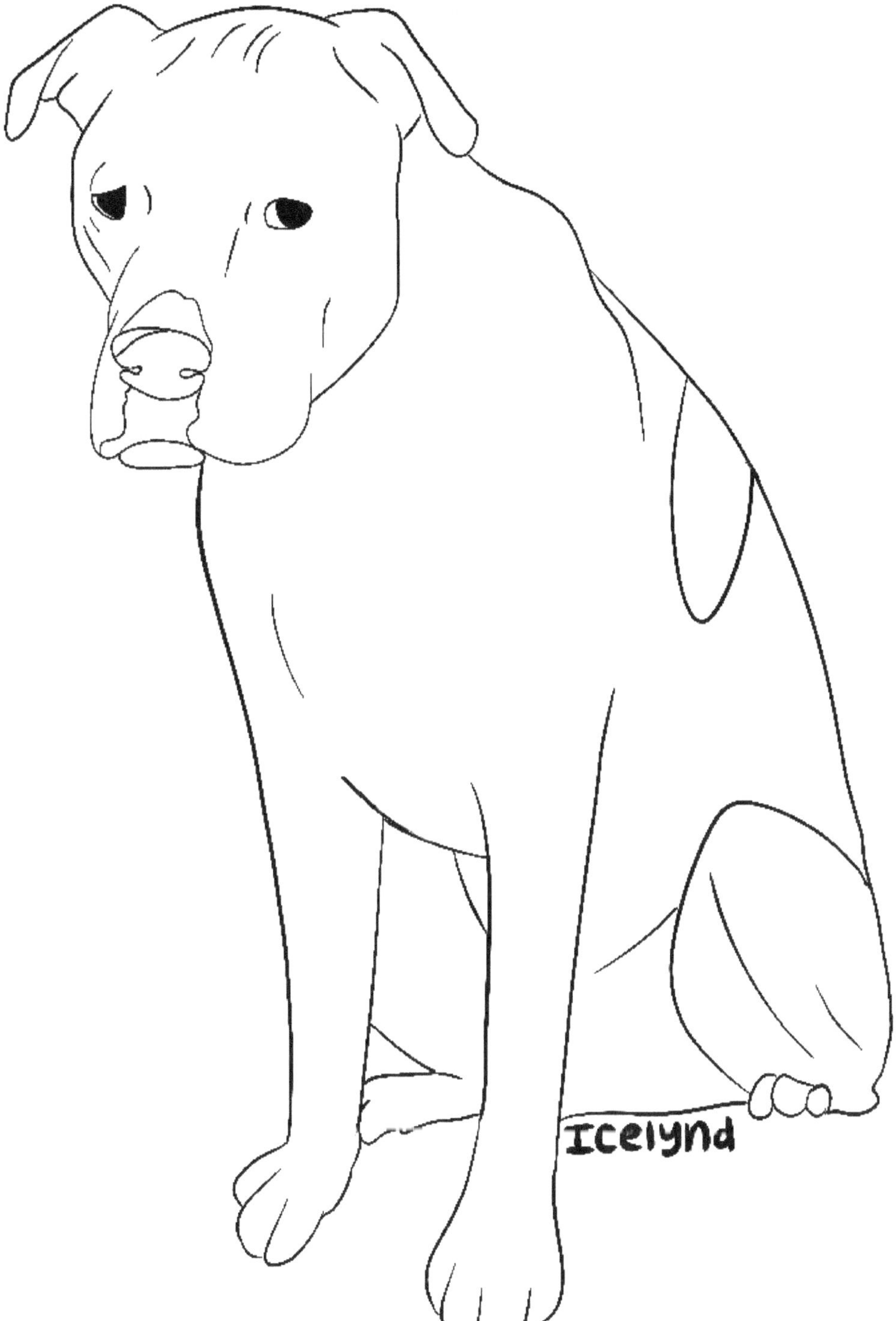
Icelynd

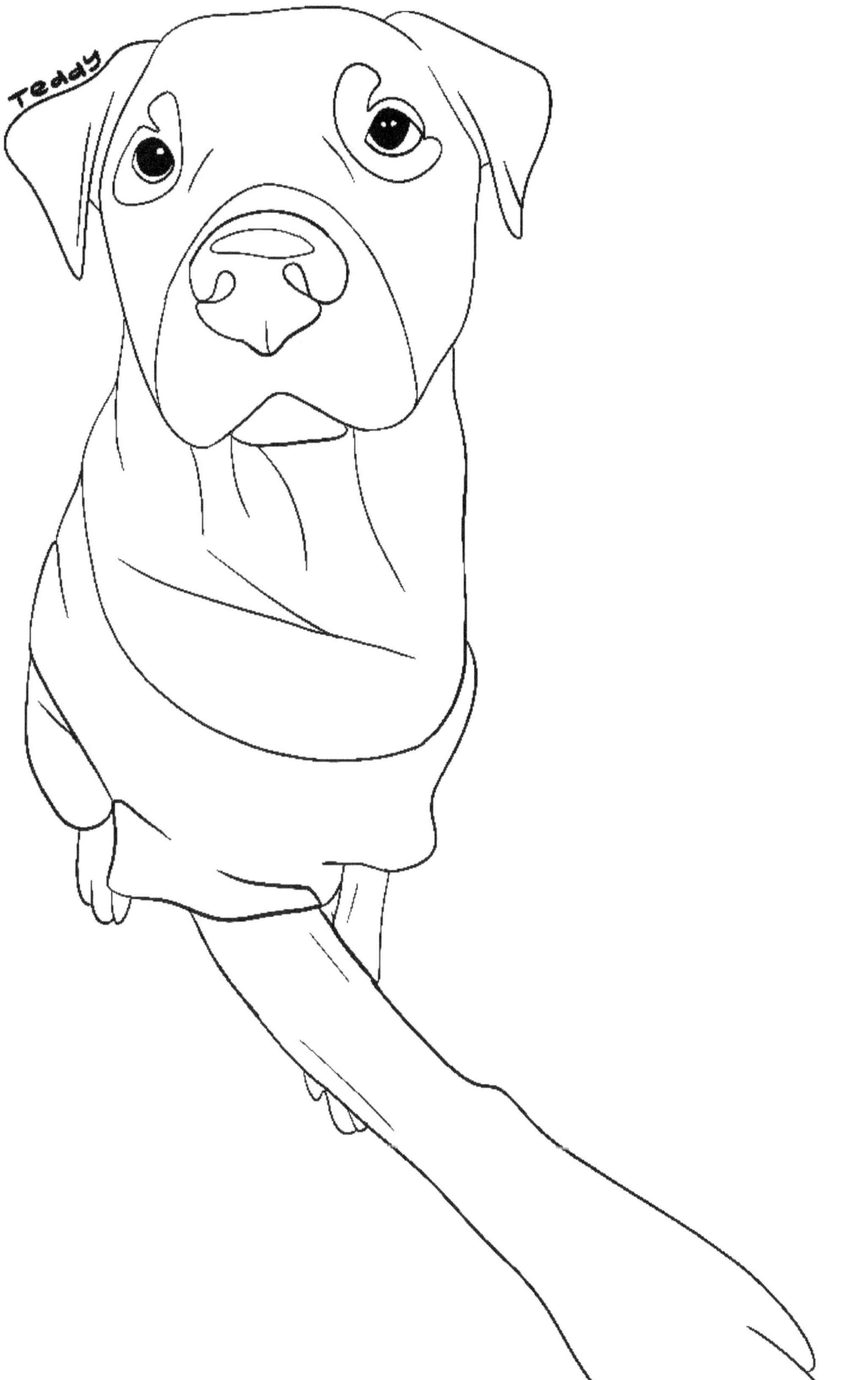
Teddy

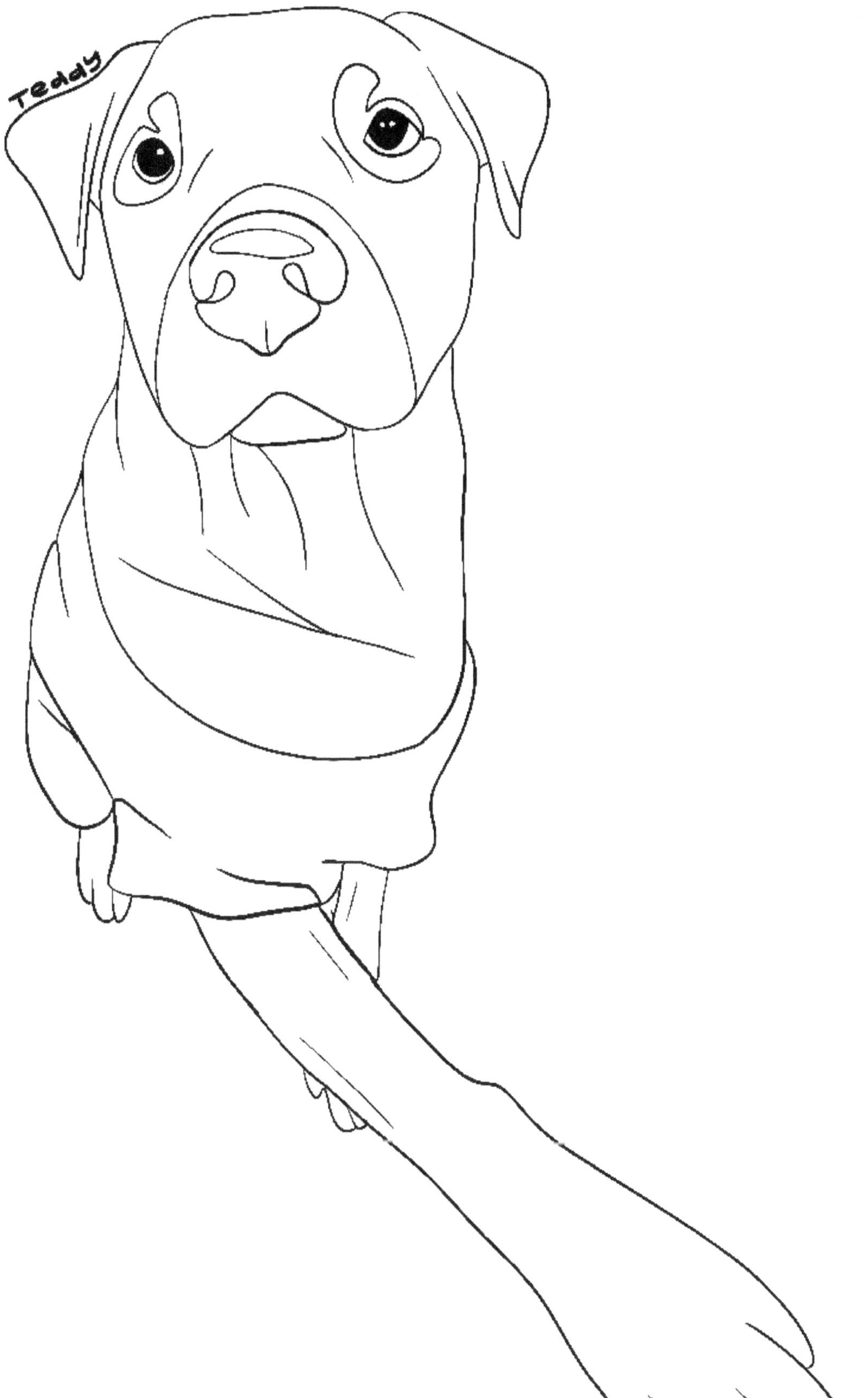
Teddy

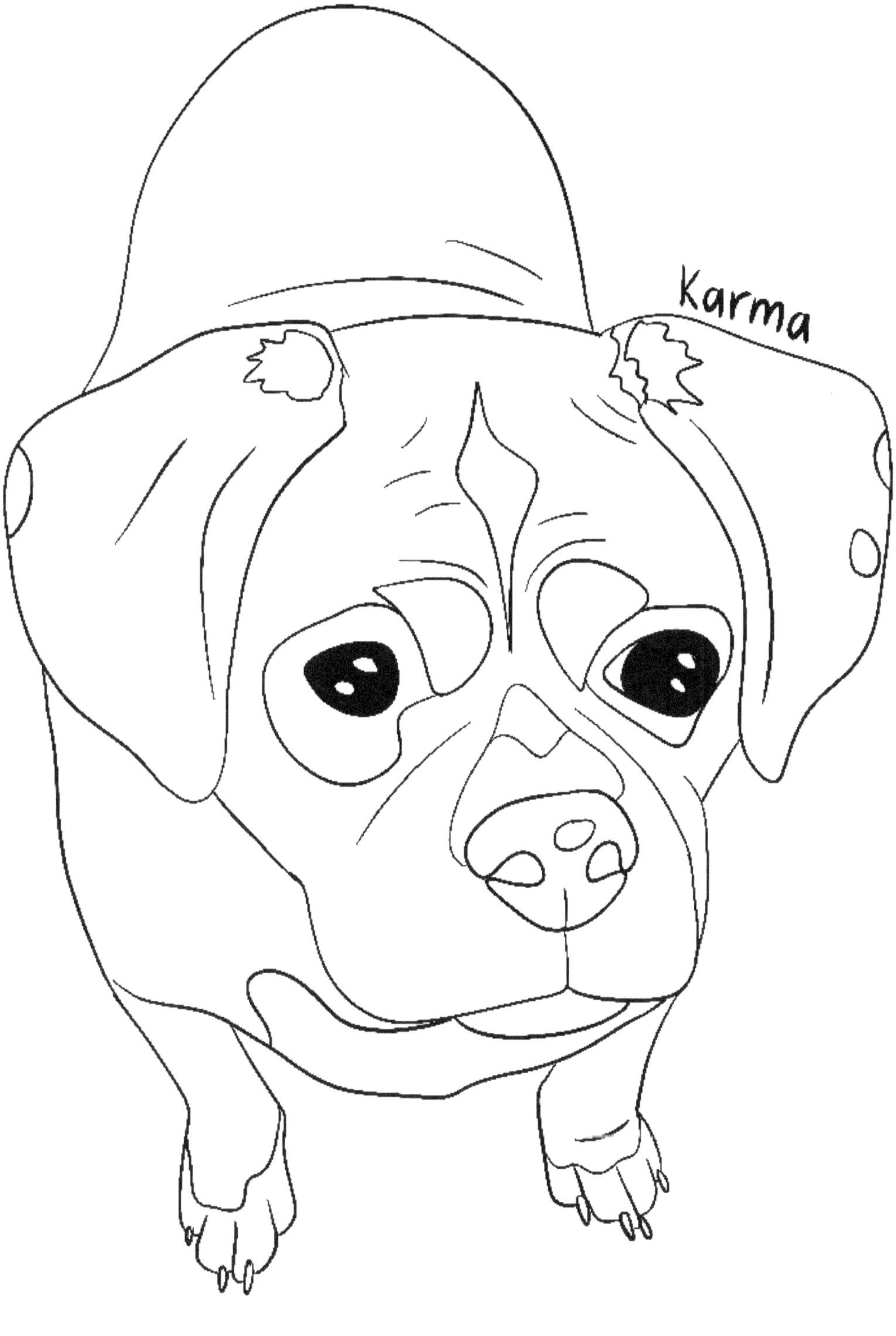
Karma

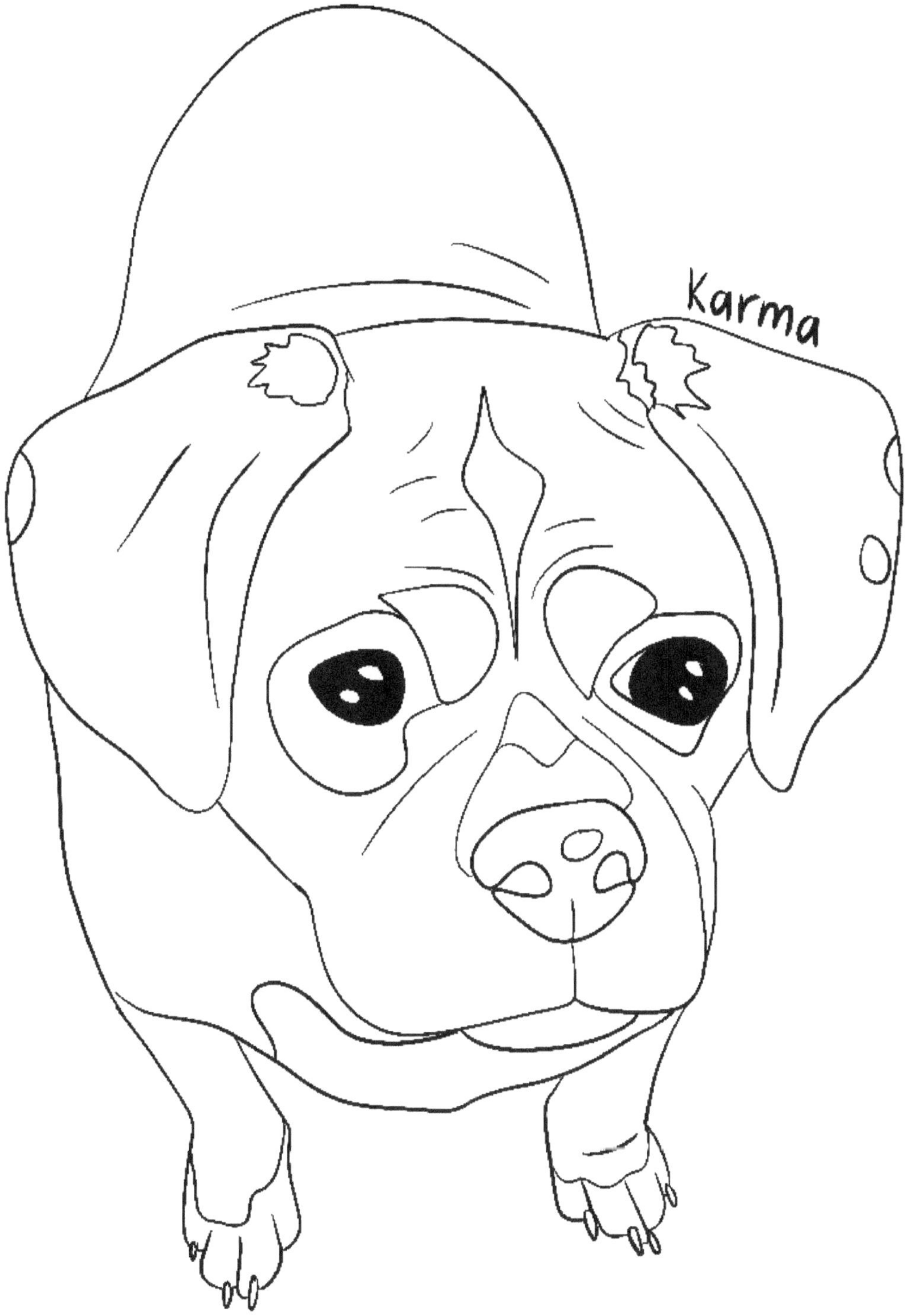
Karma

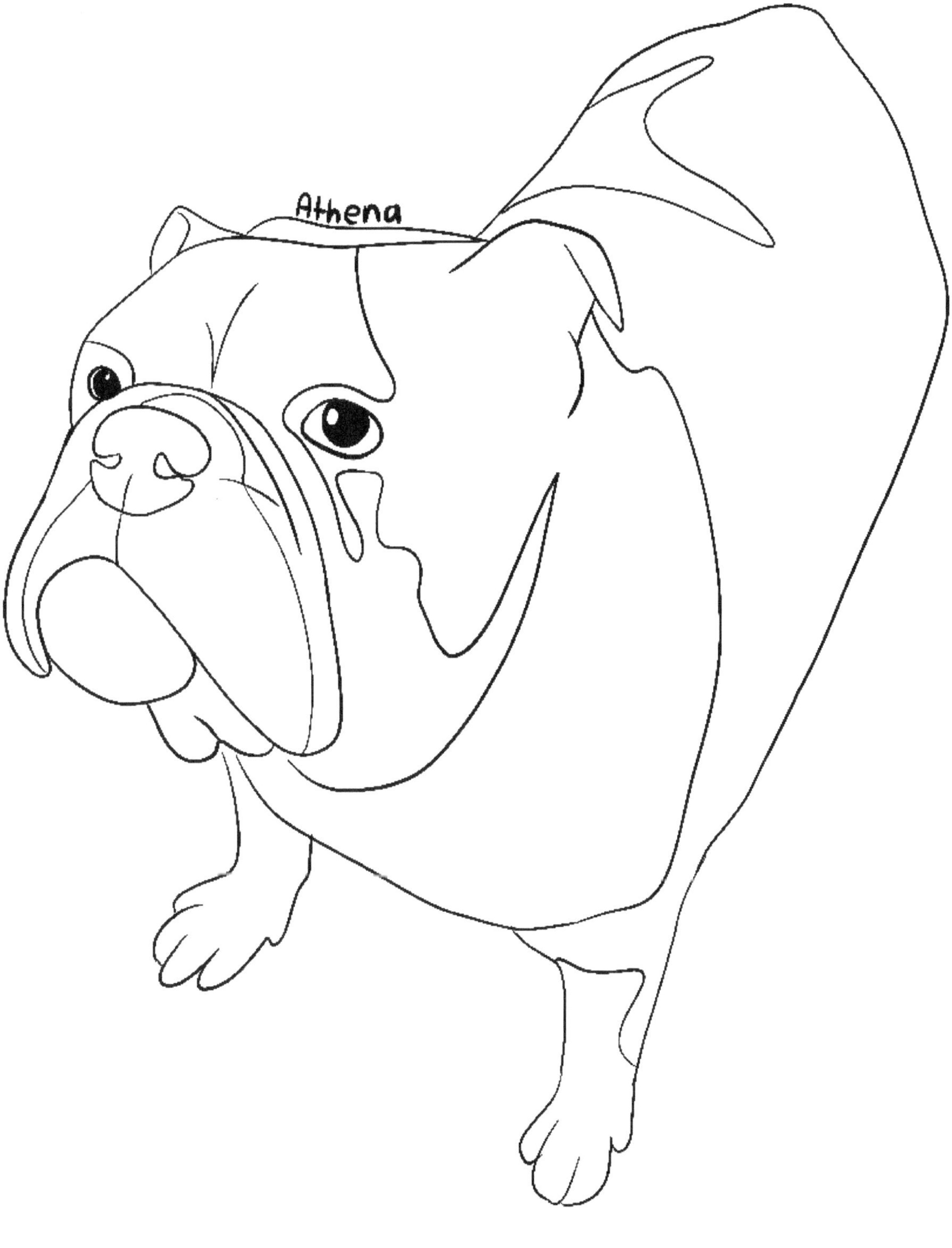
Athena

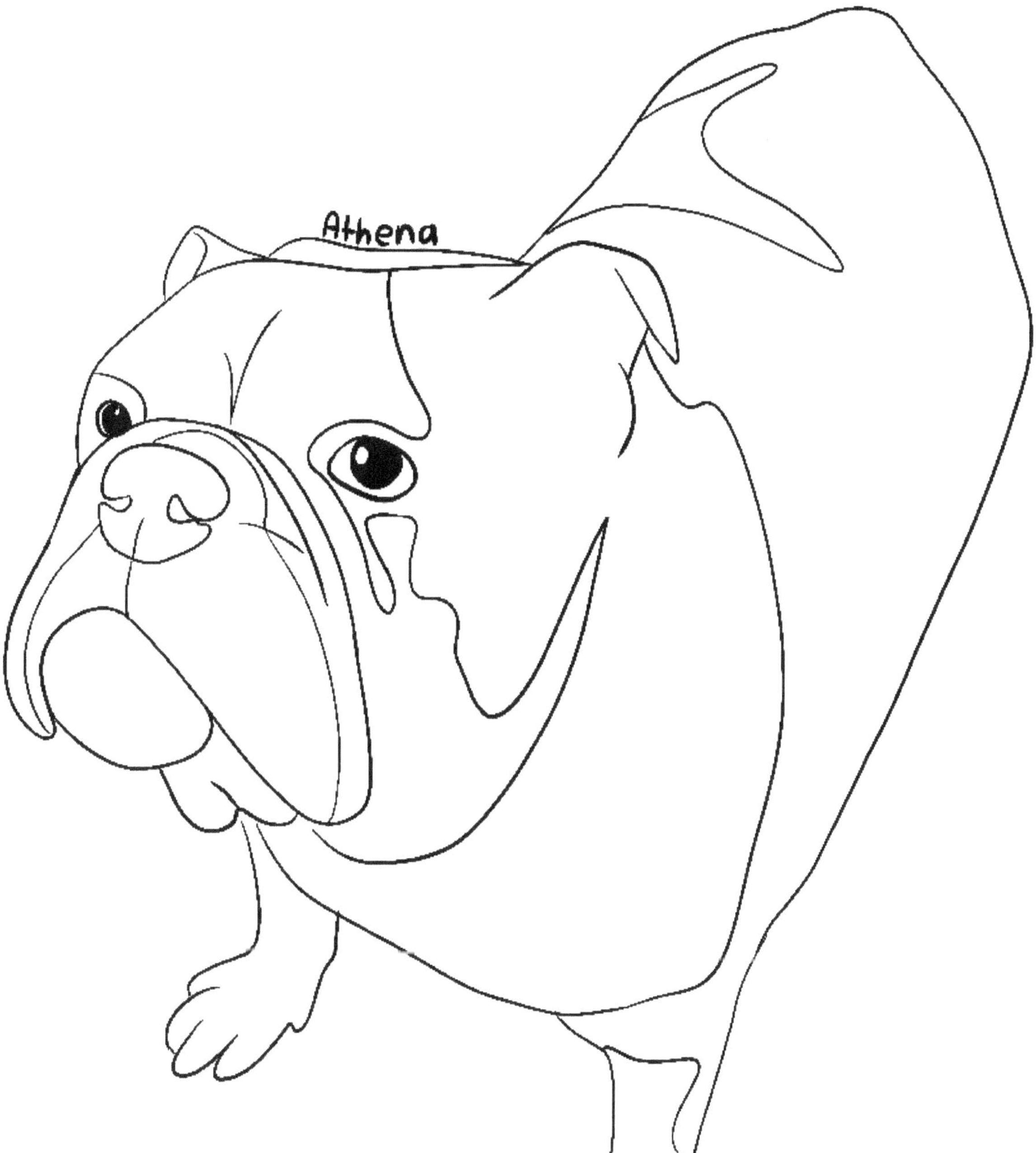
Athena

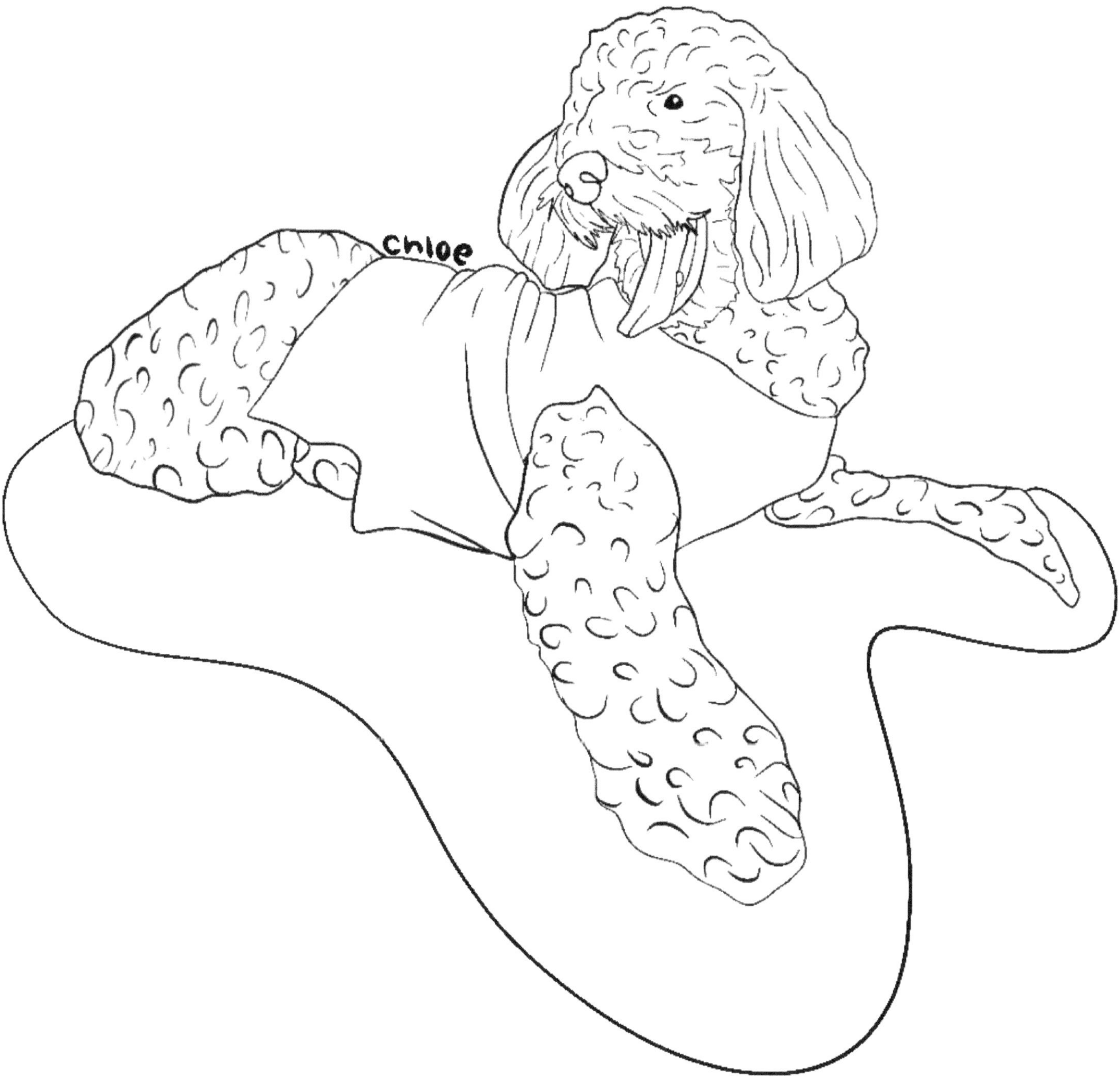
Chloe

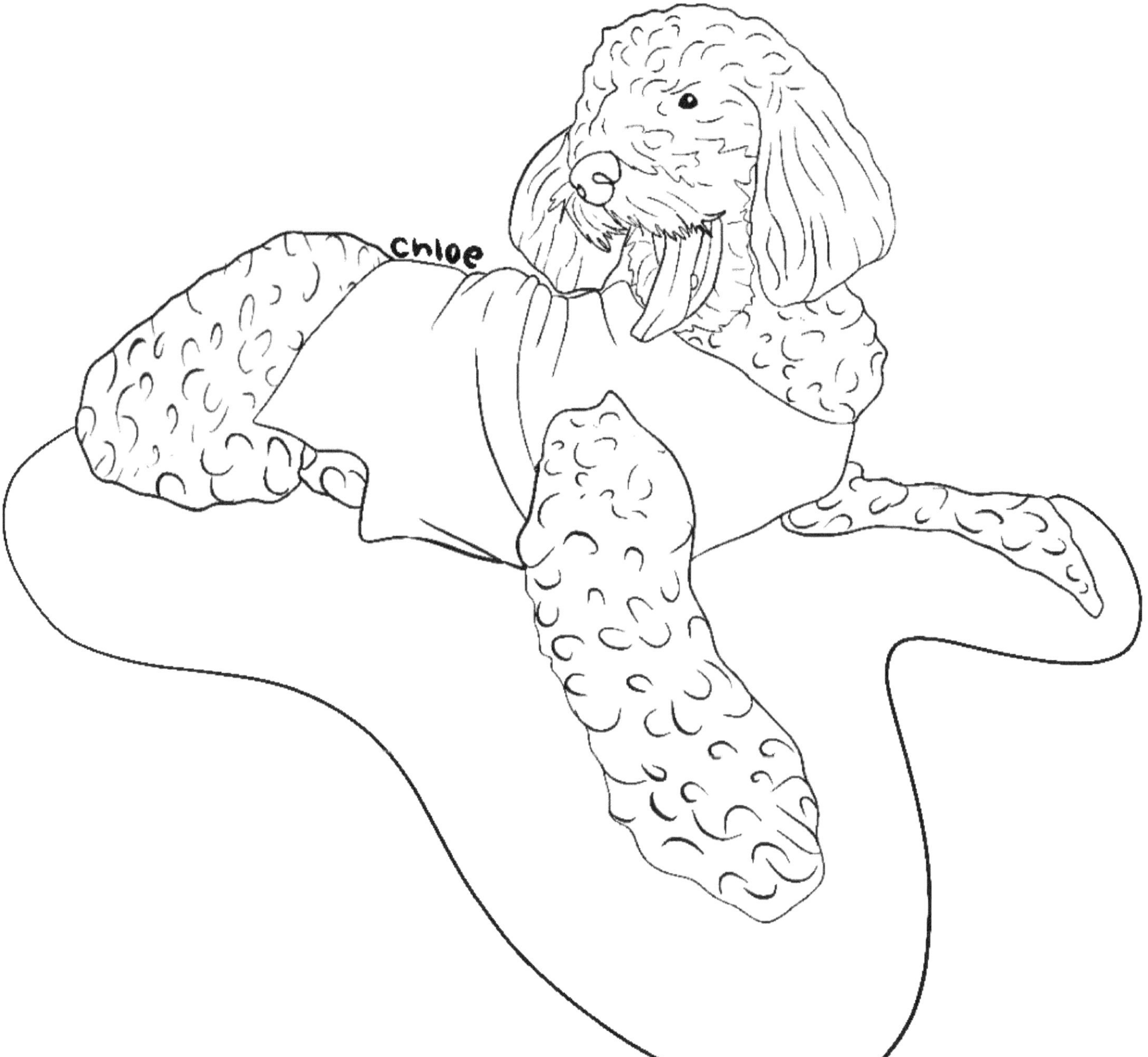
Chloe

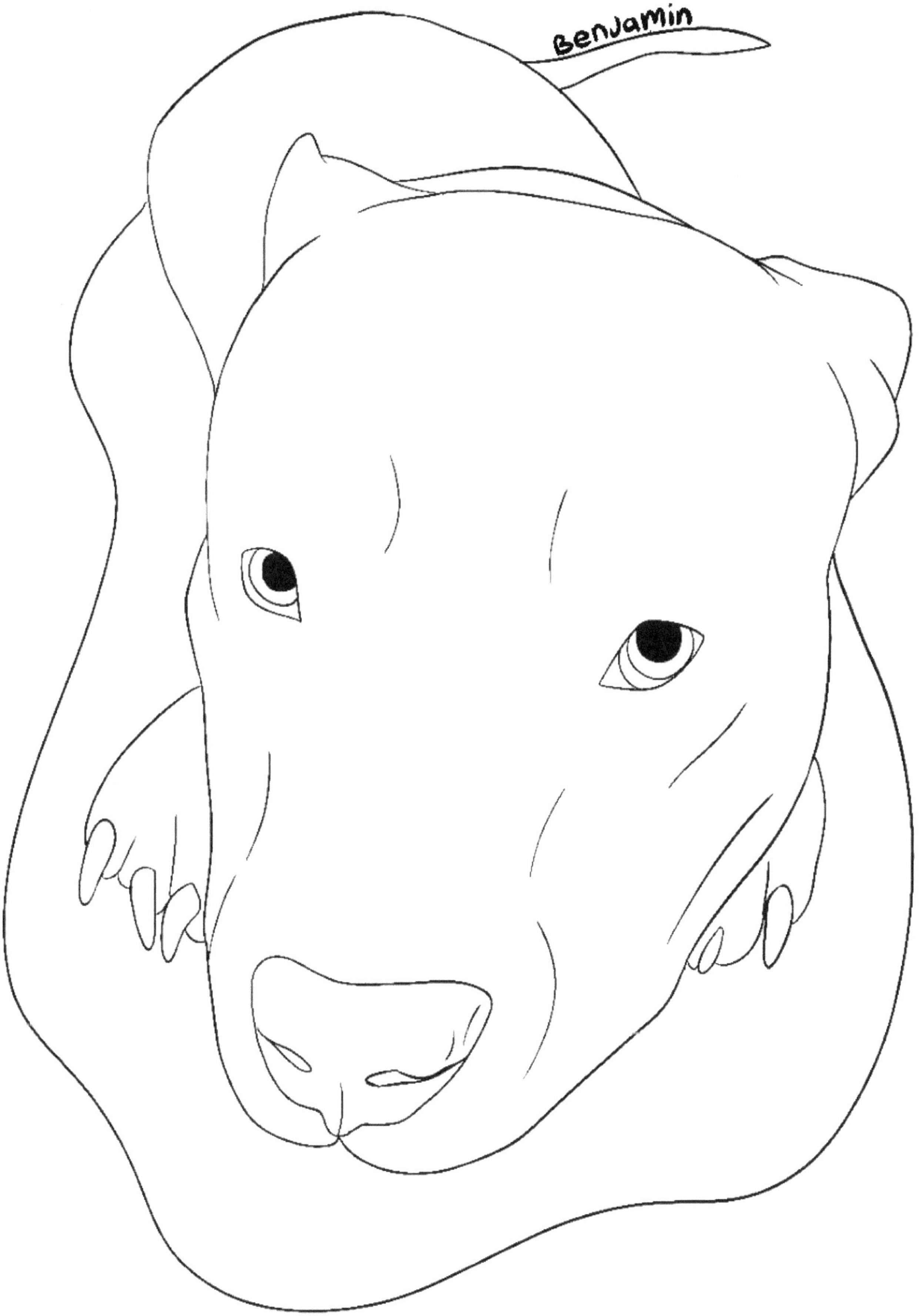
Benjamin

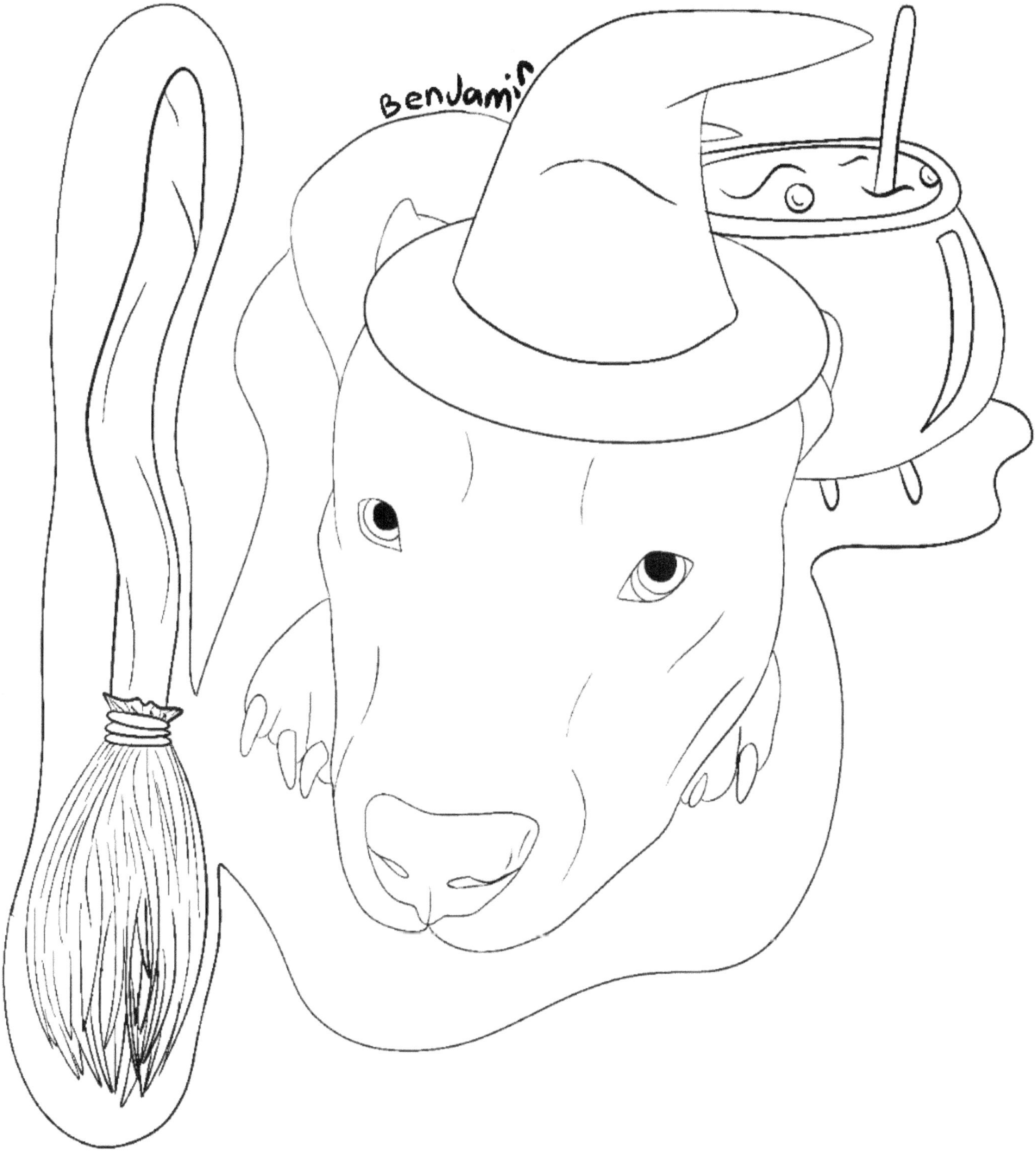
BenJamin

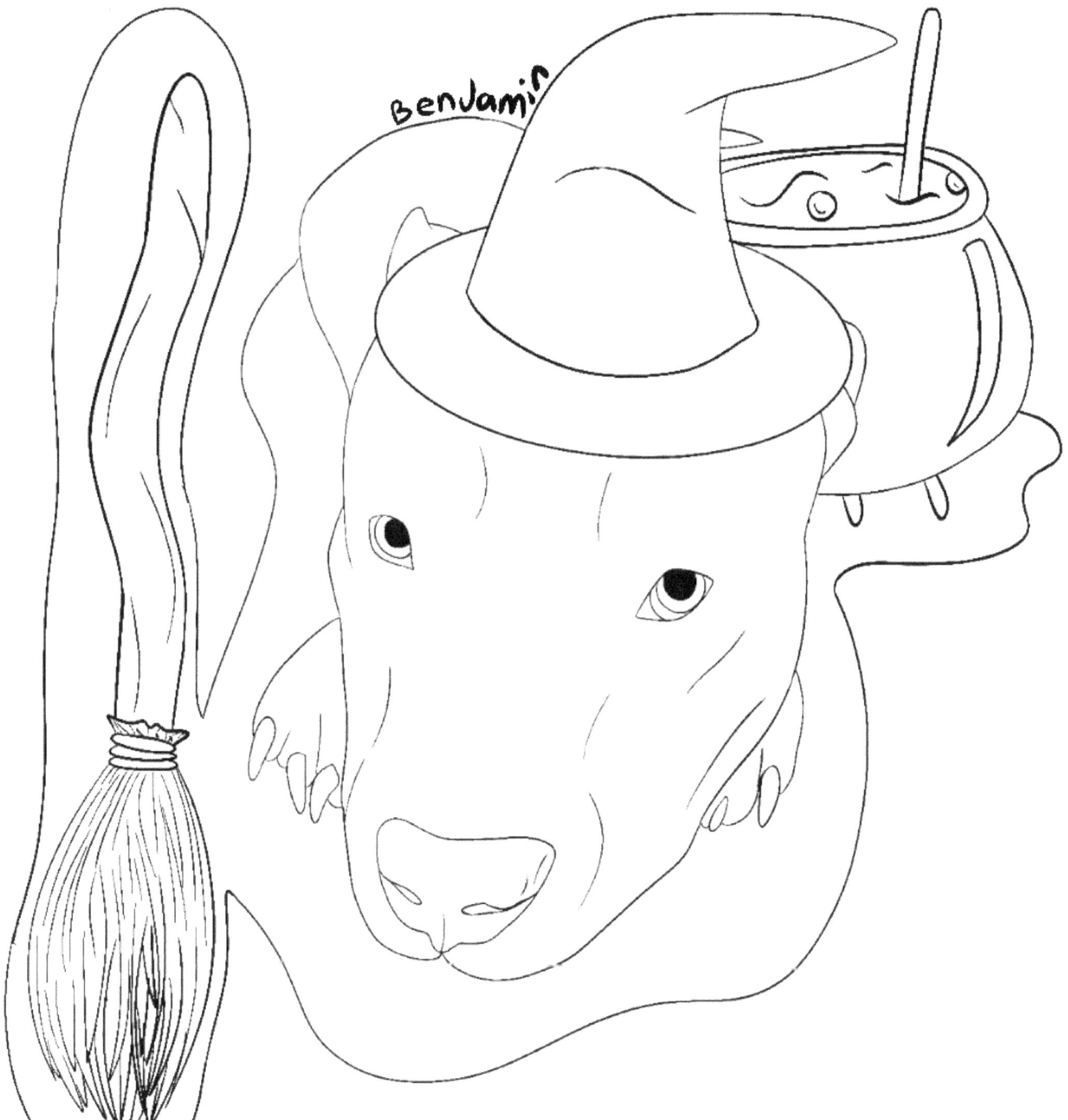
BenJamin

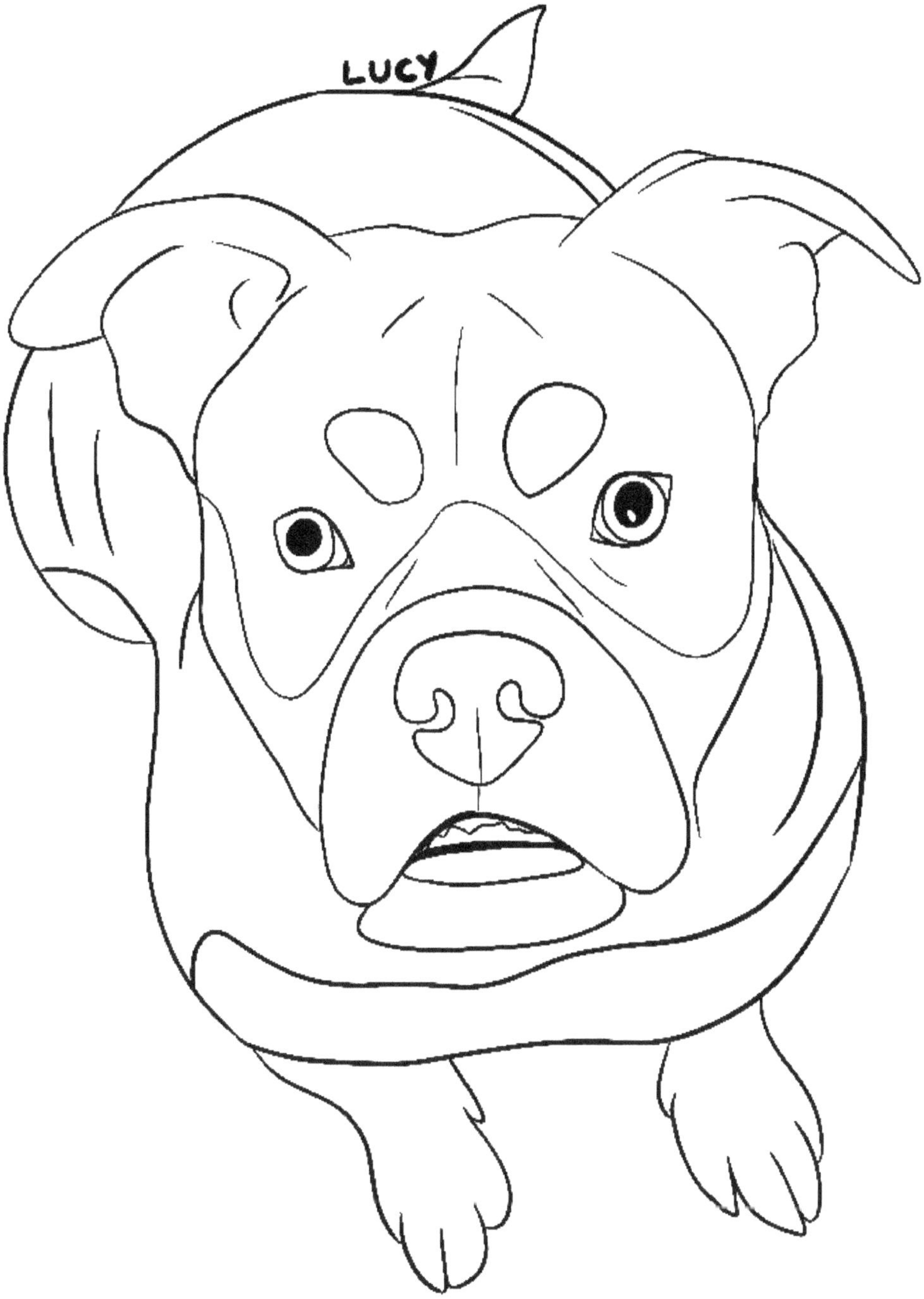
LUCY

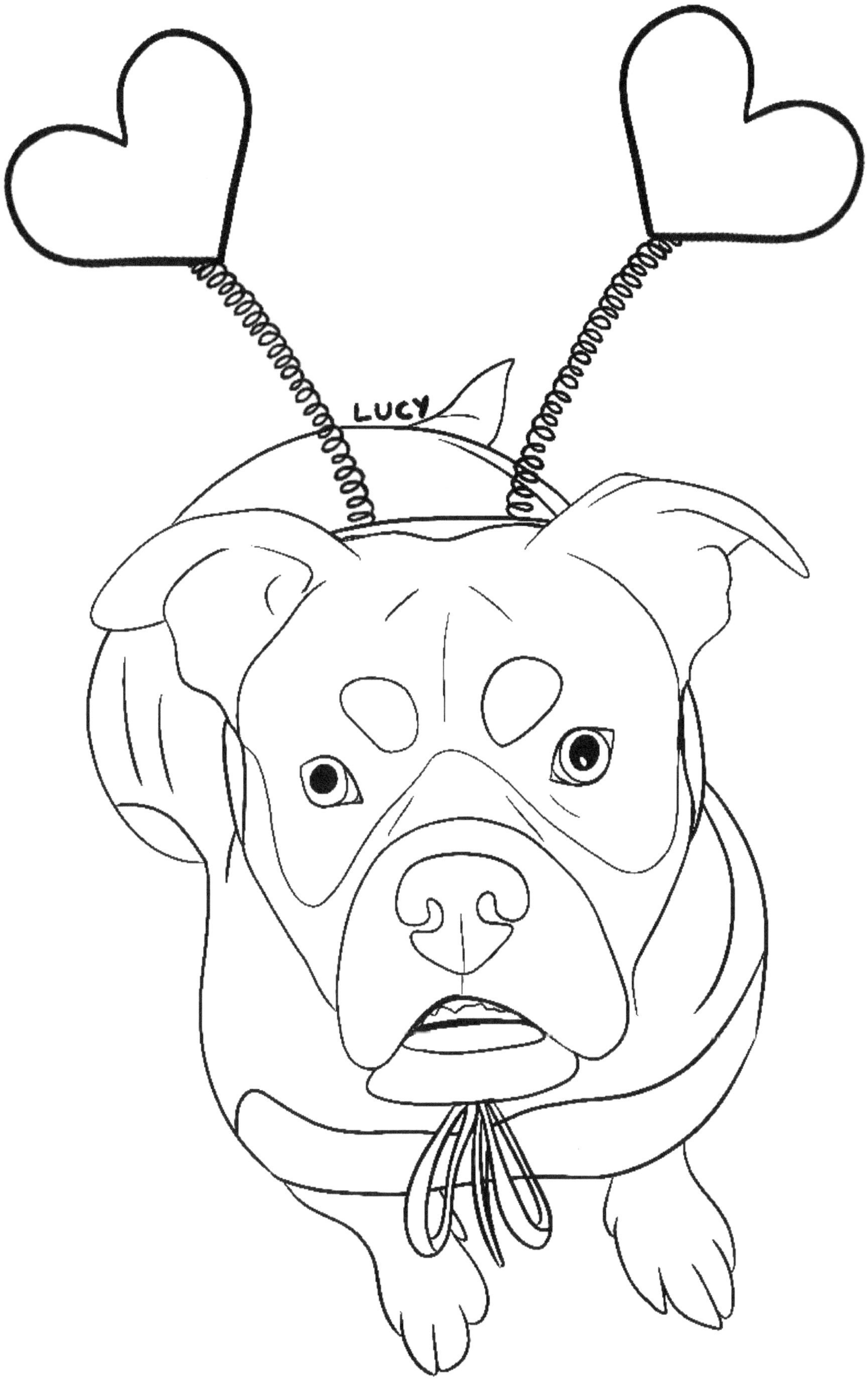
LUCY

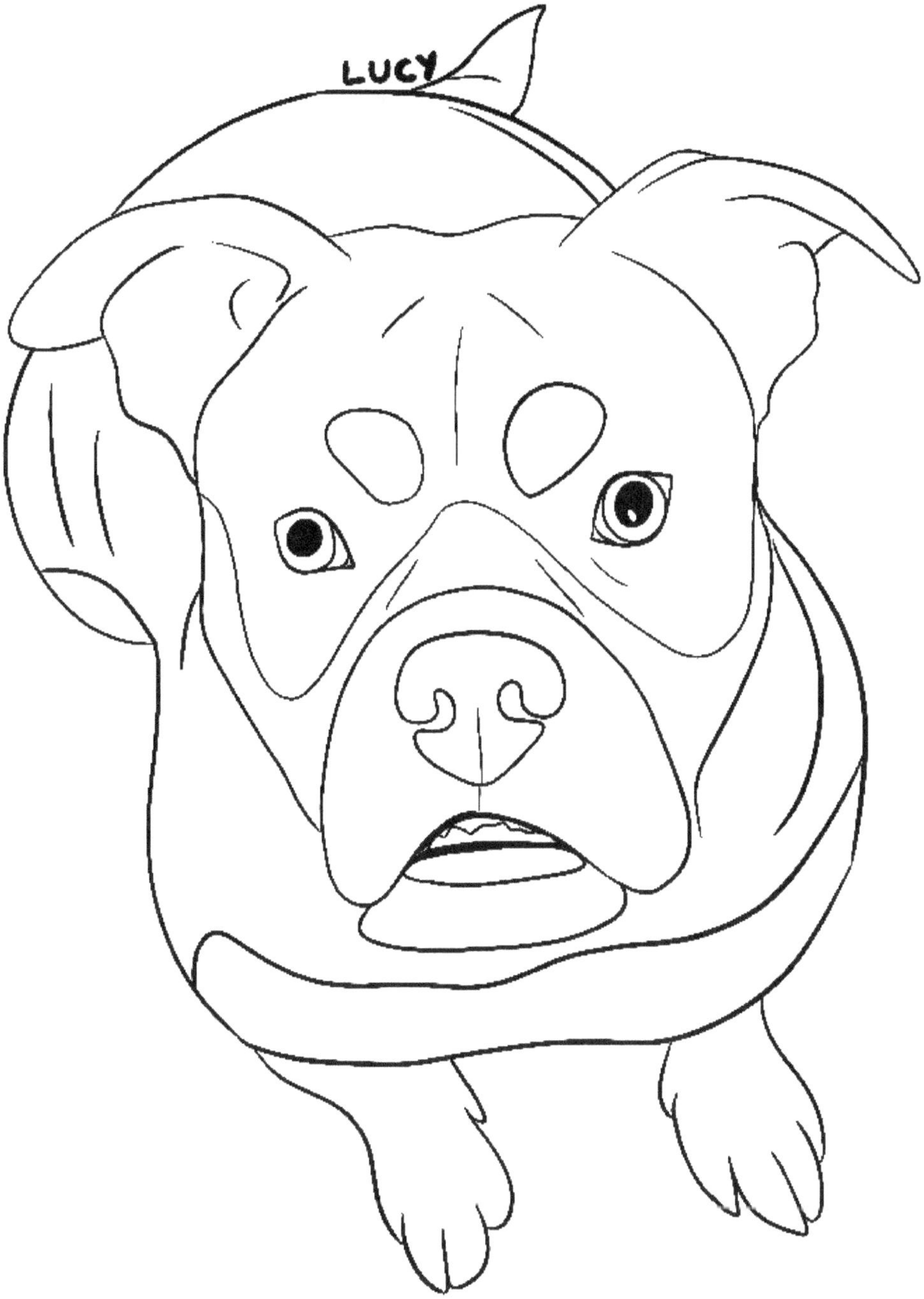
LUCY

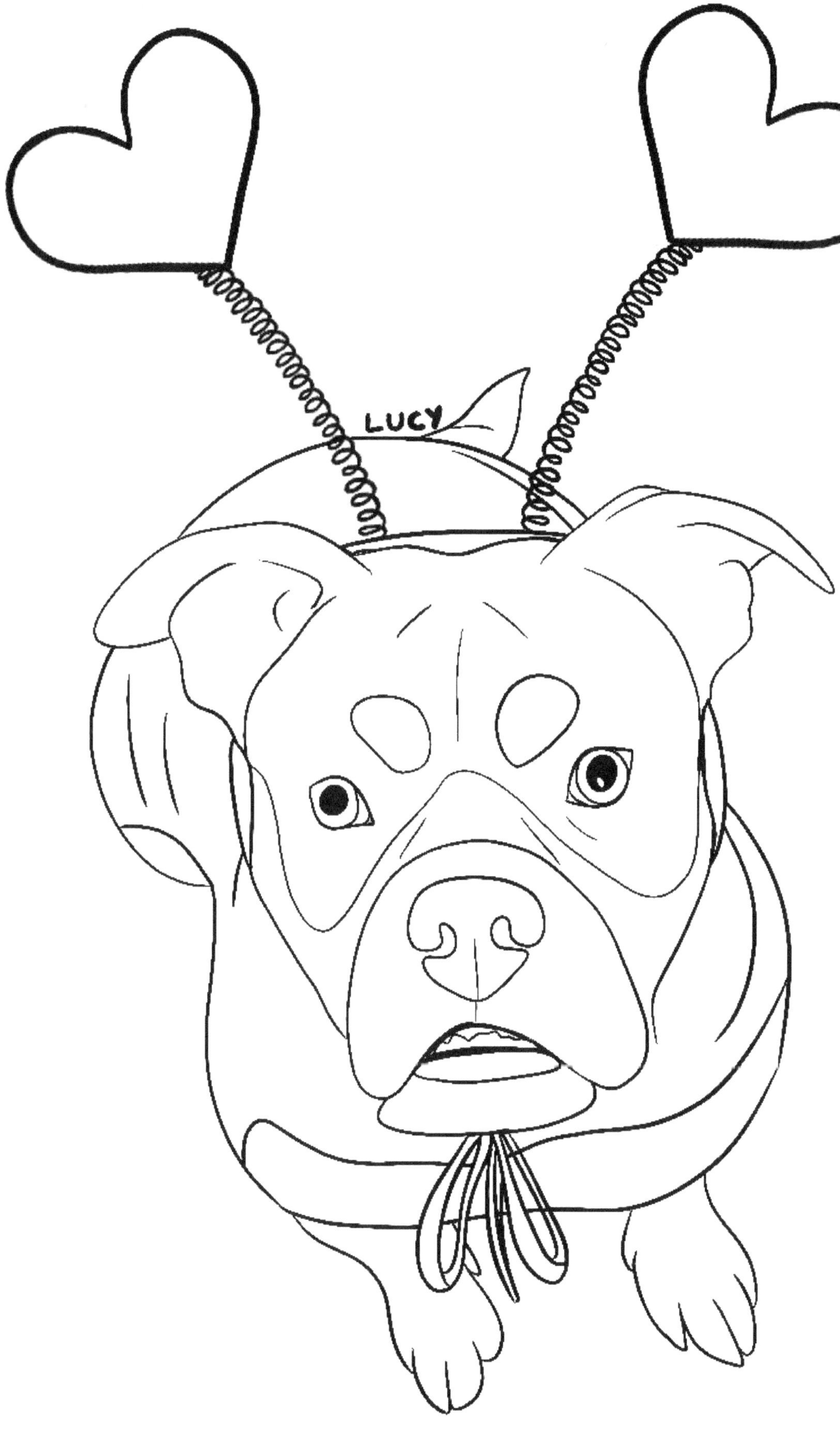
LUCY

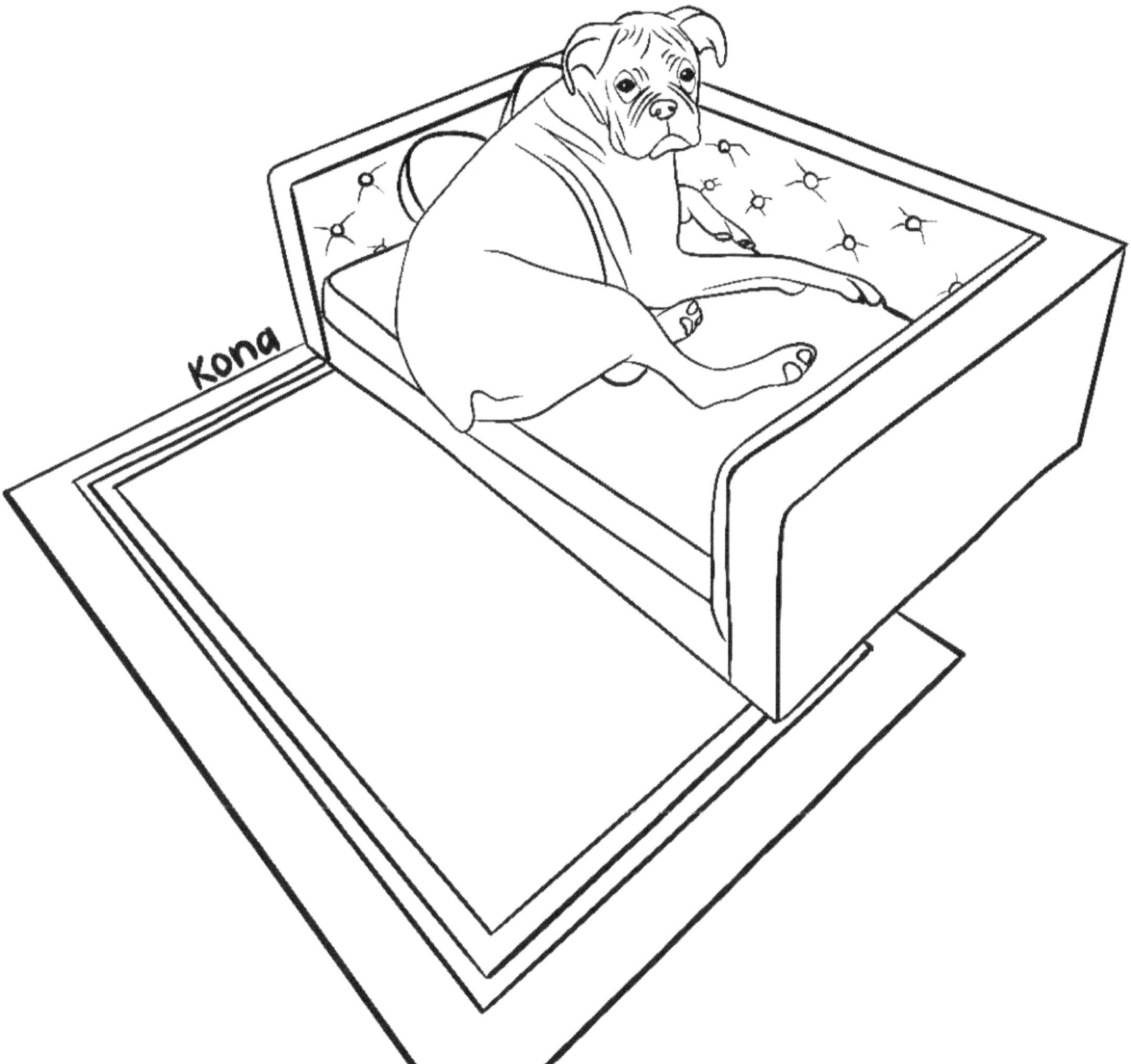
Kona

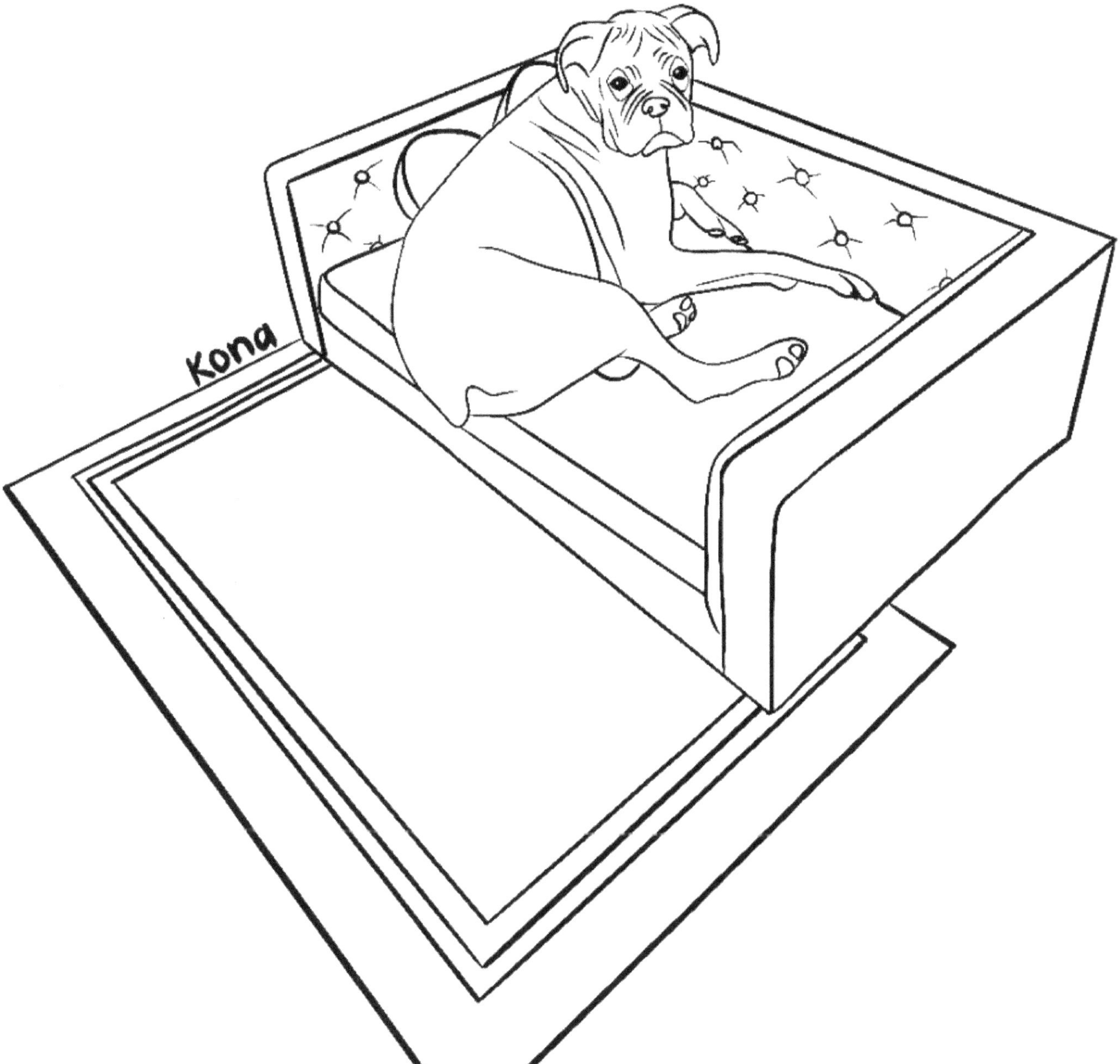
Kona

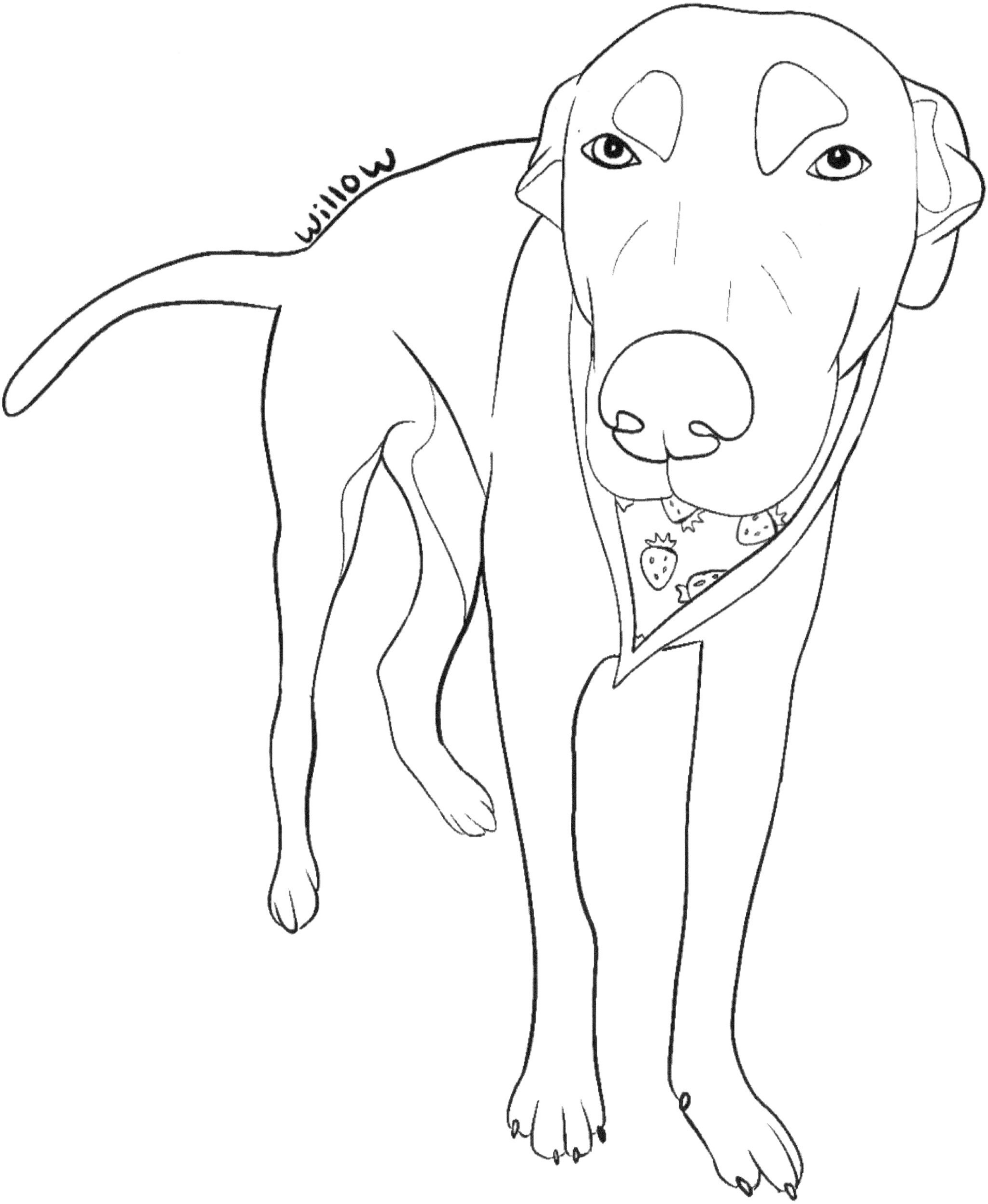
Willow

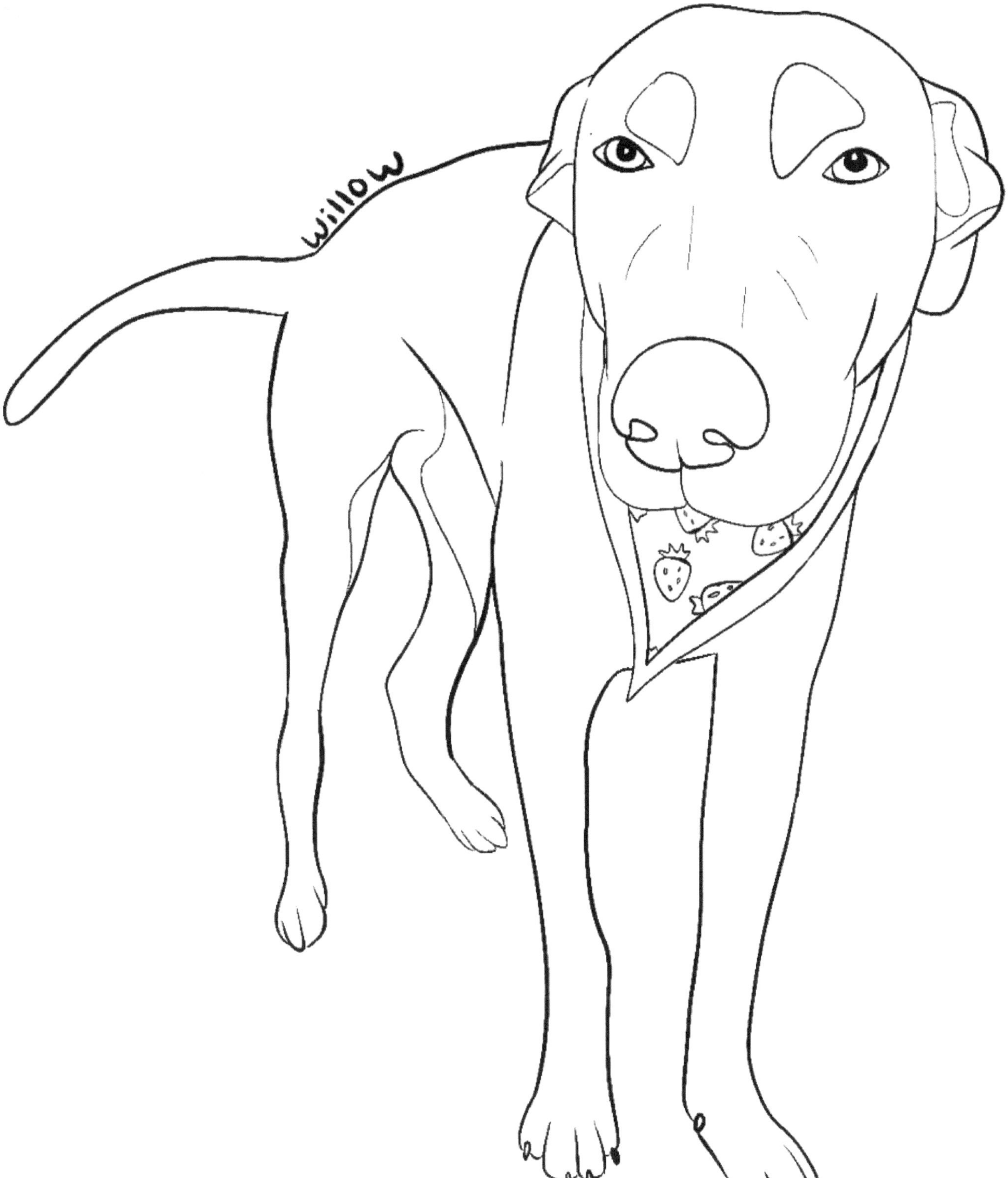
Willow

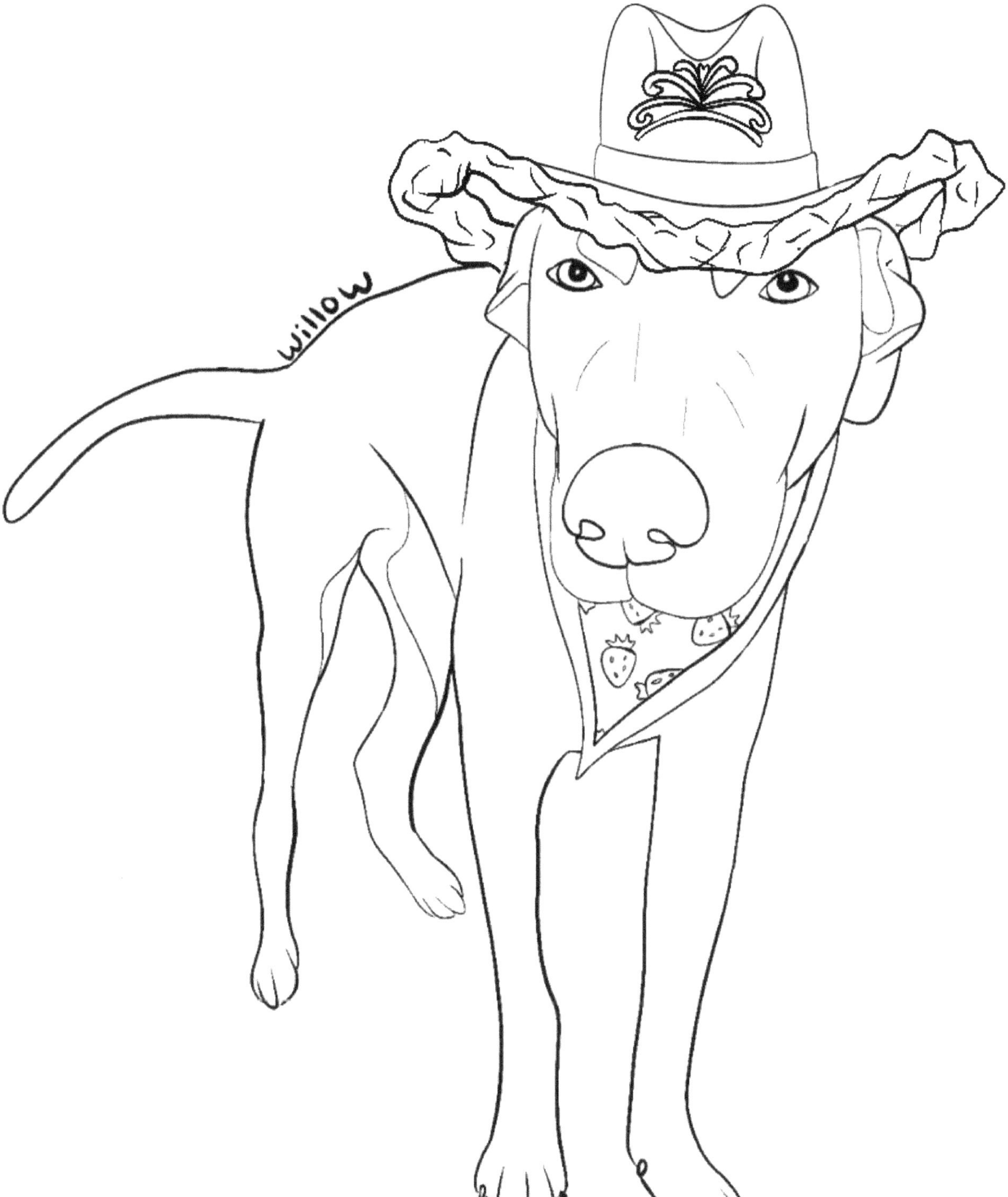
Willow

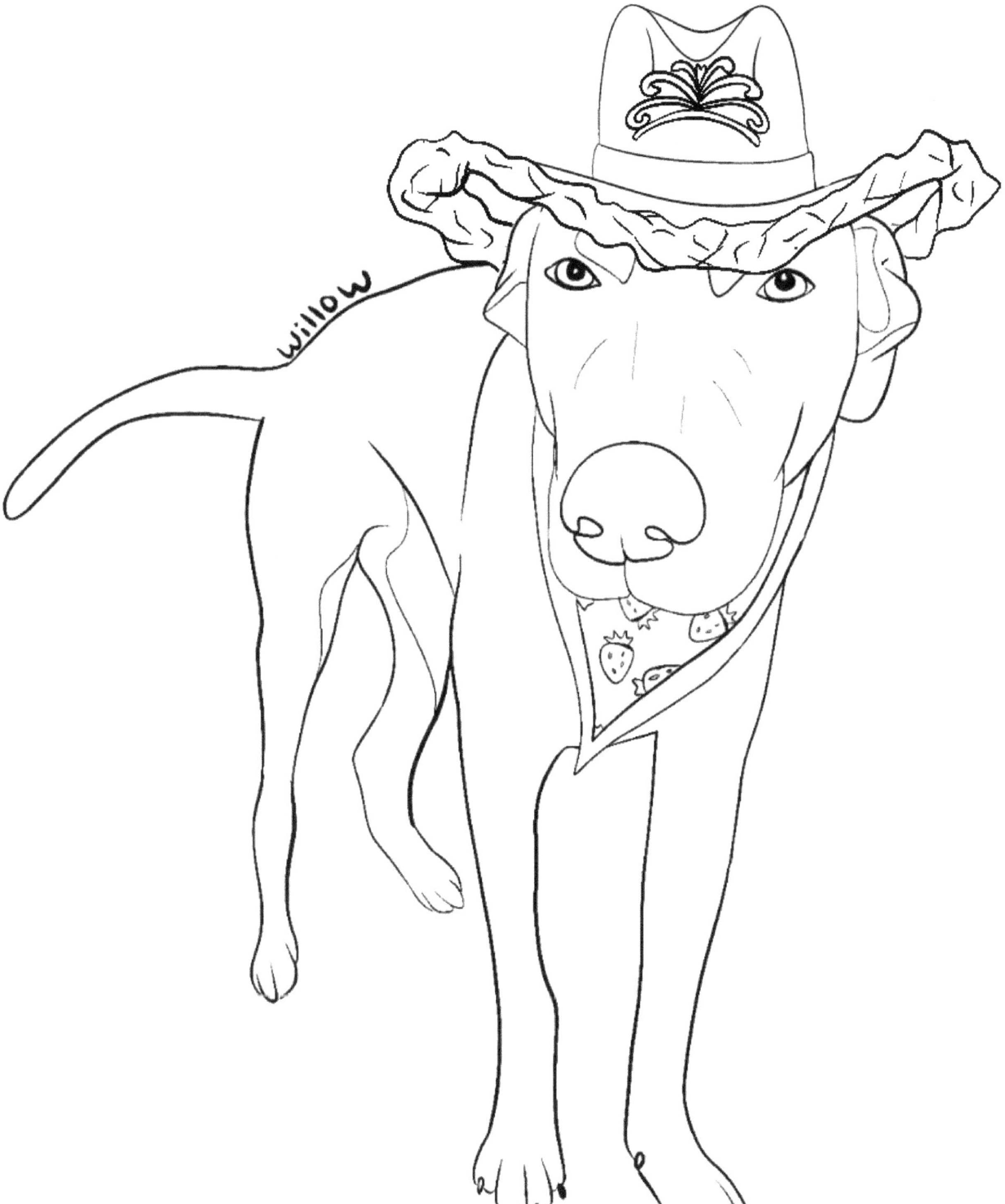
willow

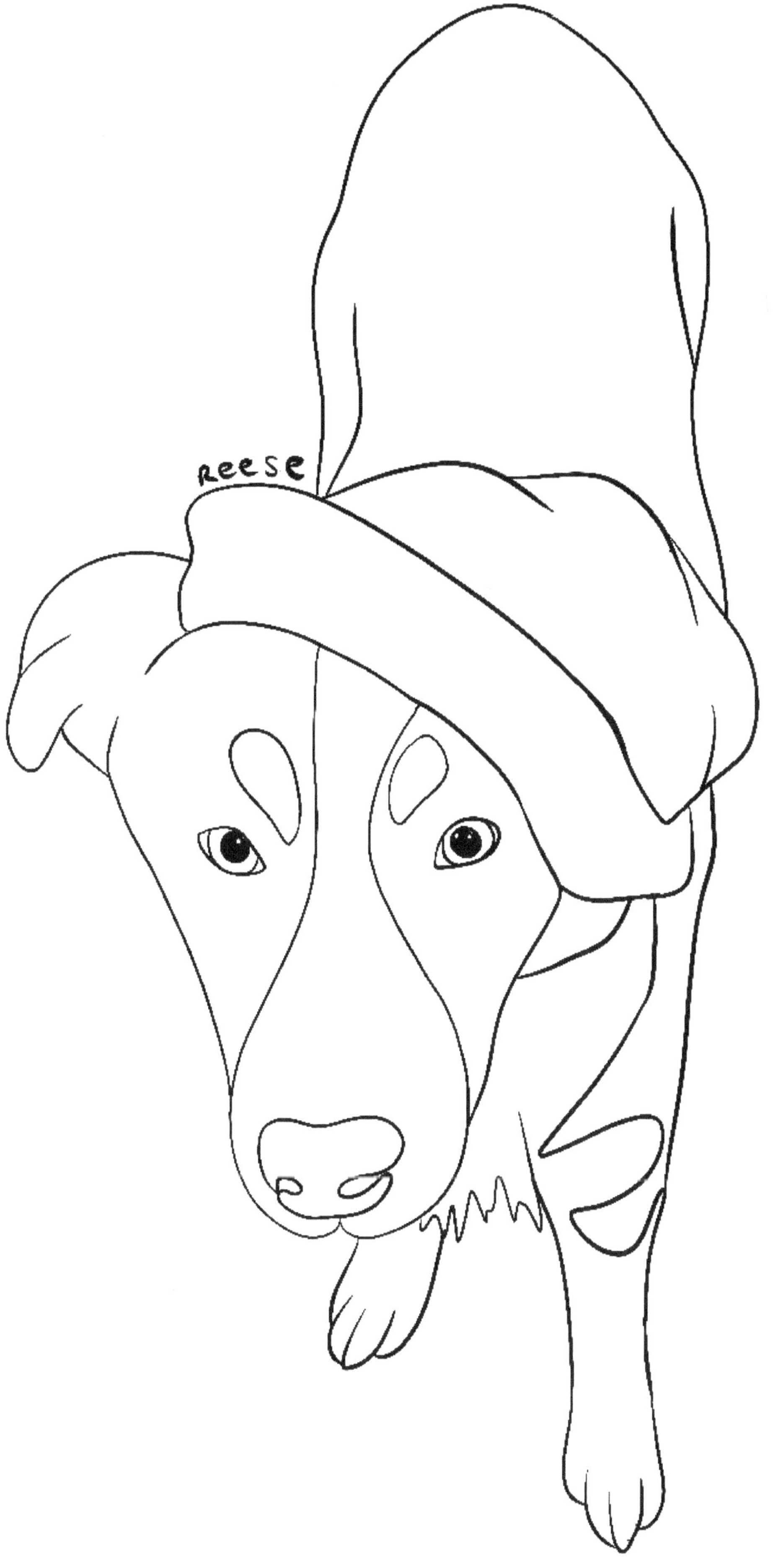
Reese

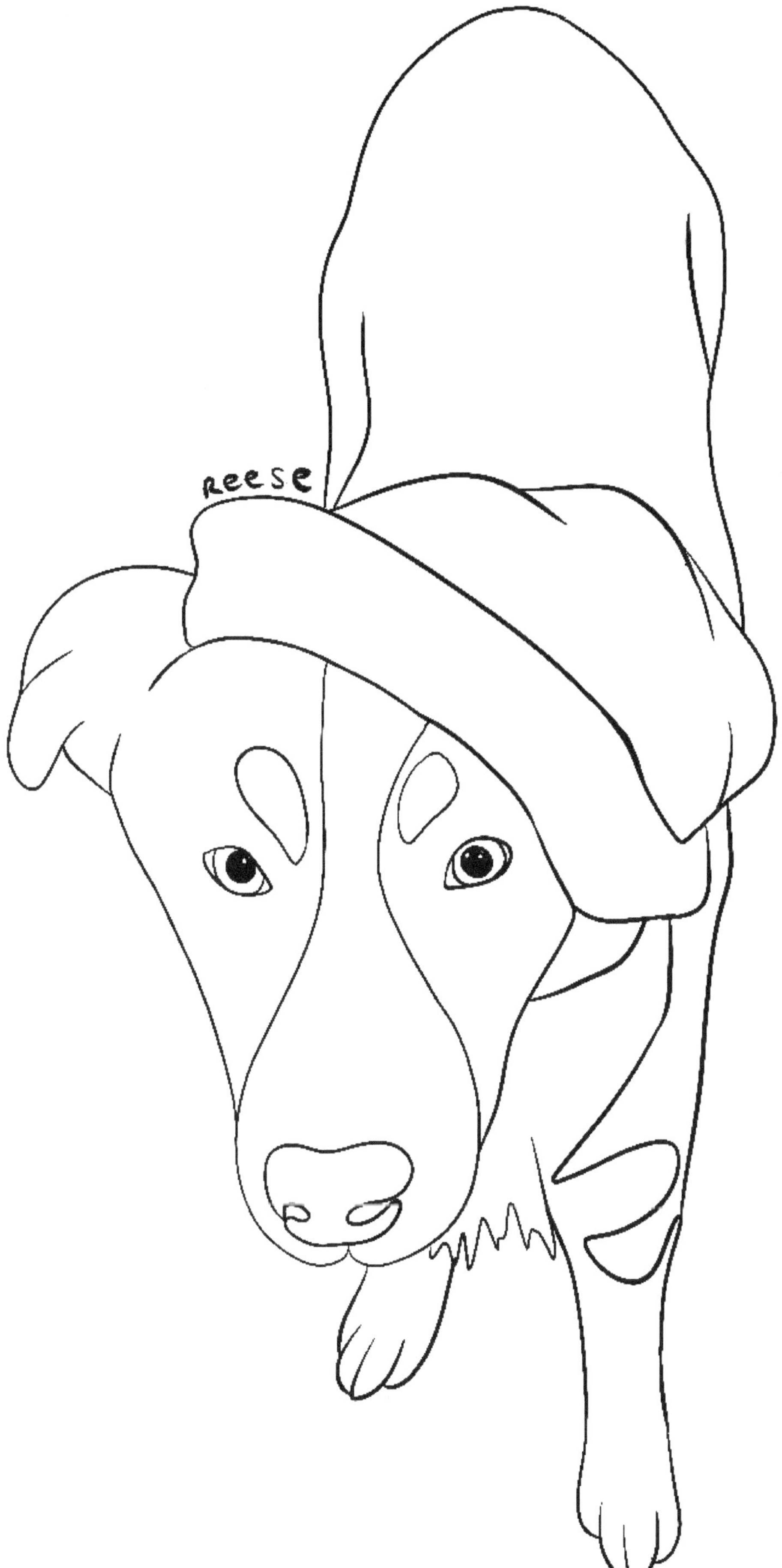
Reese

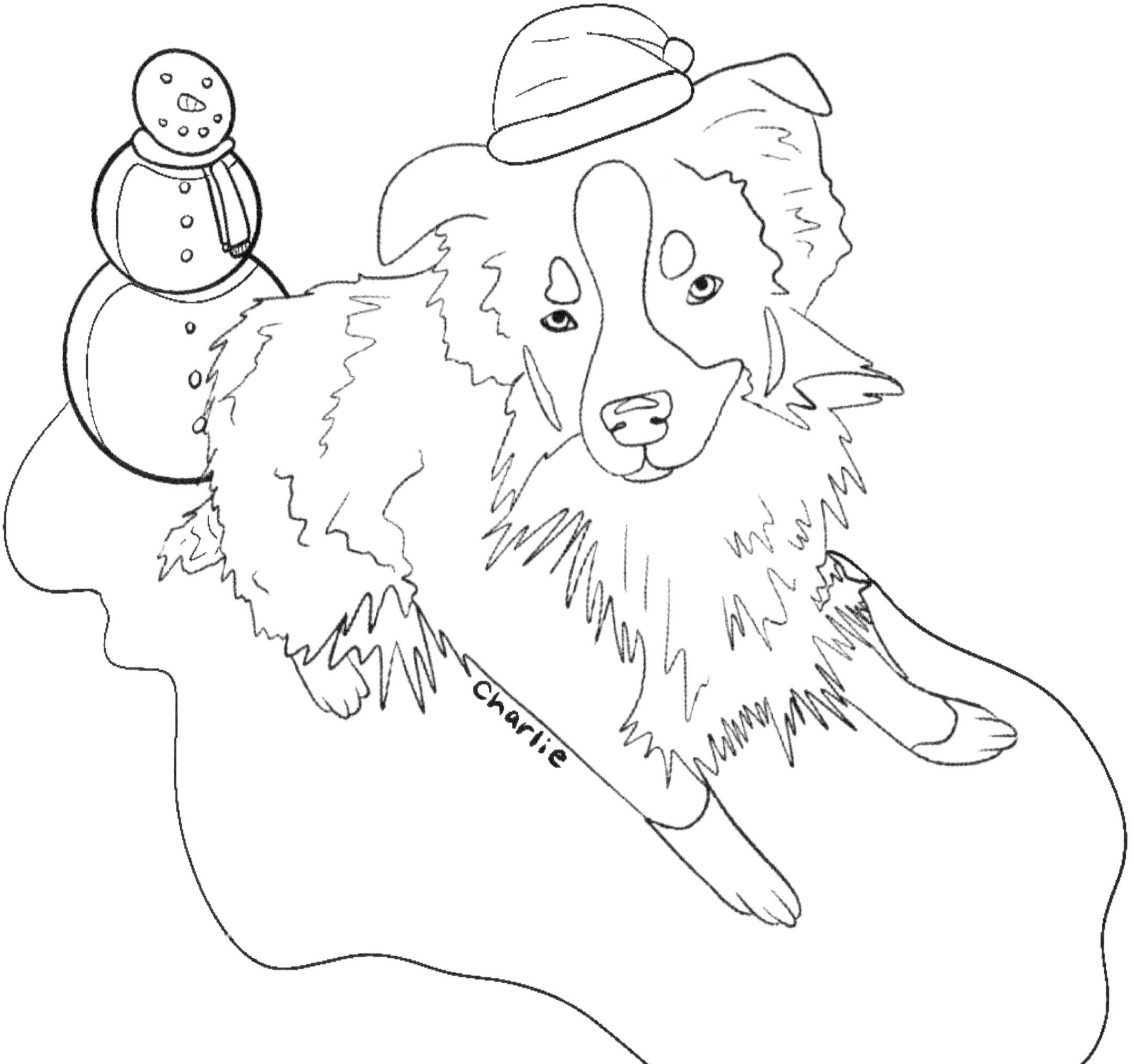
Charlie

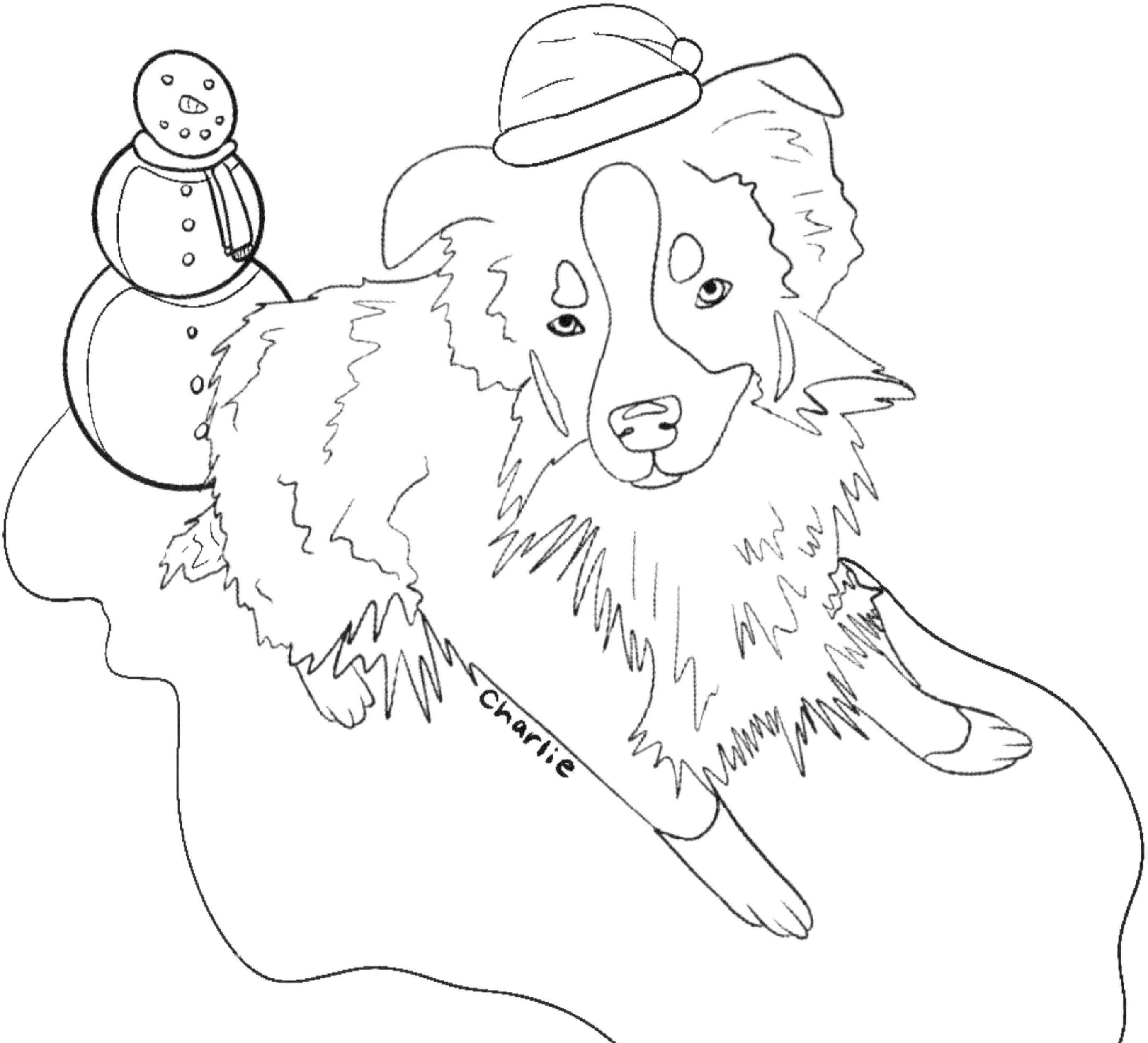
Charlie

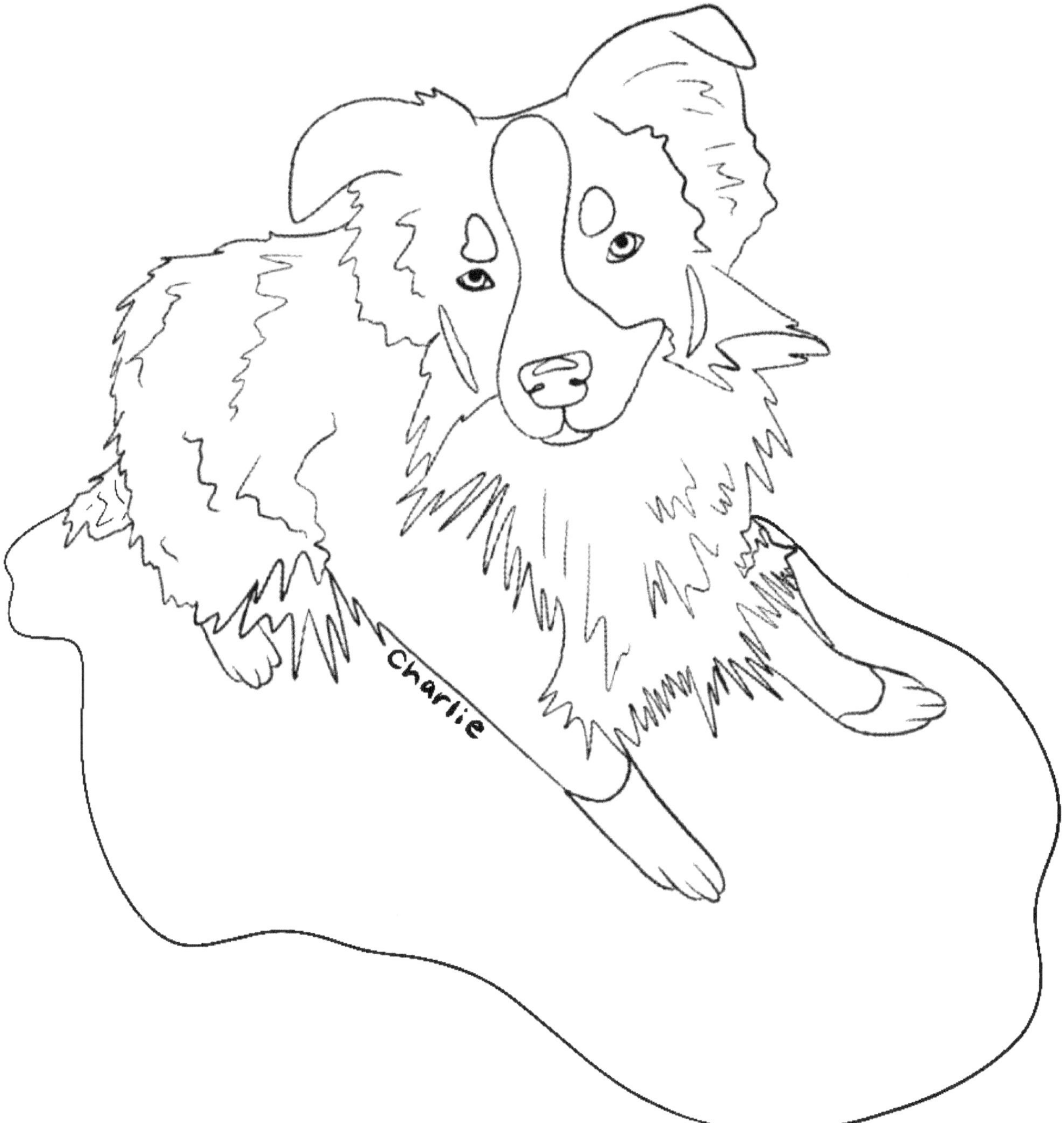
Charlie

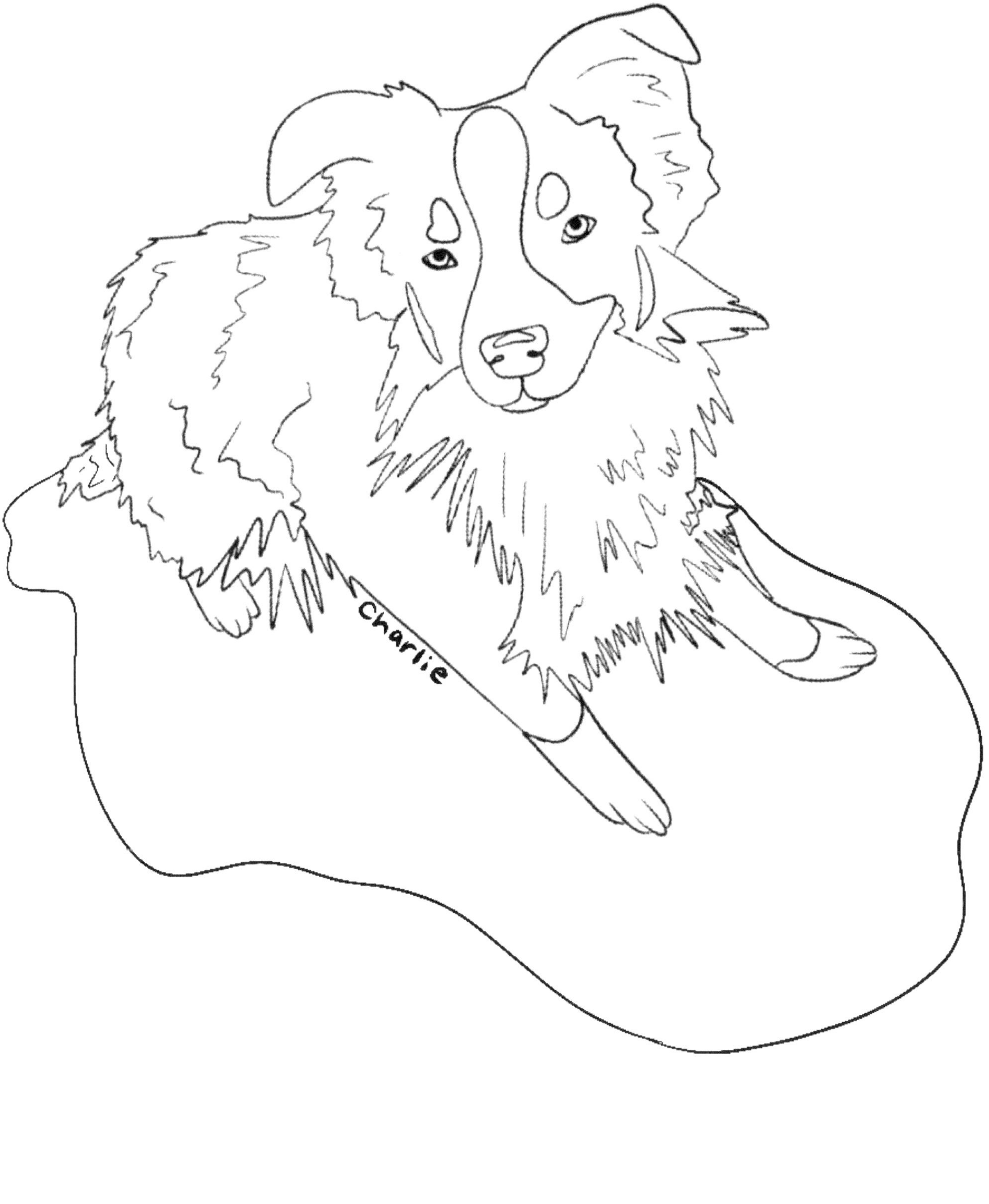
Charlie

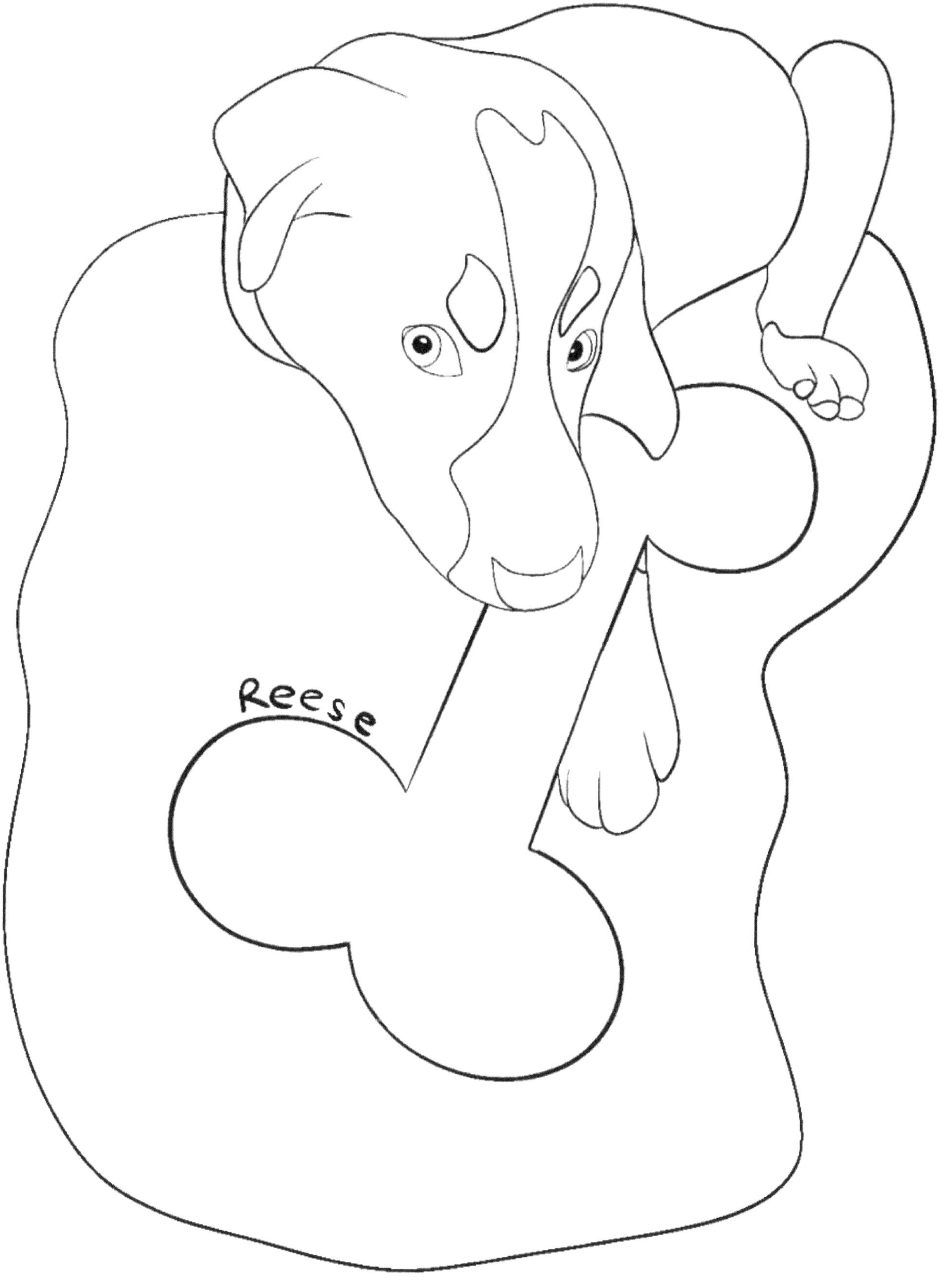
Reese

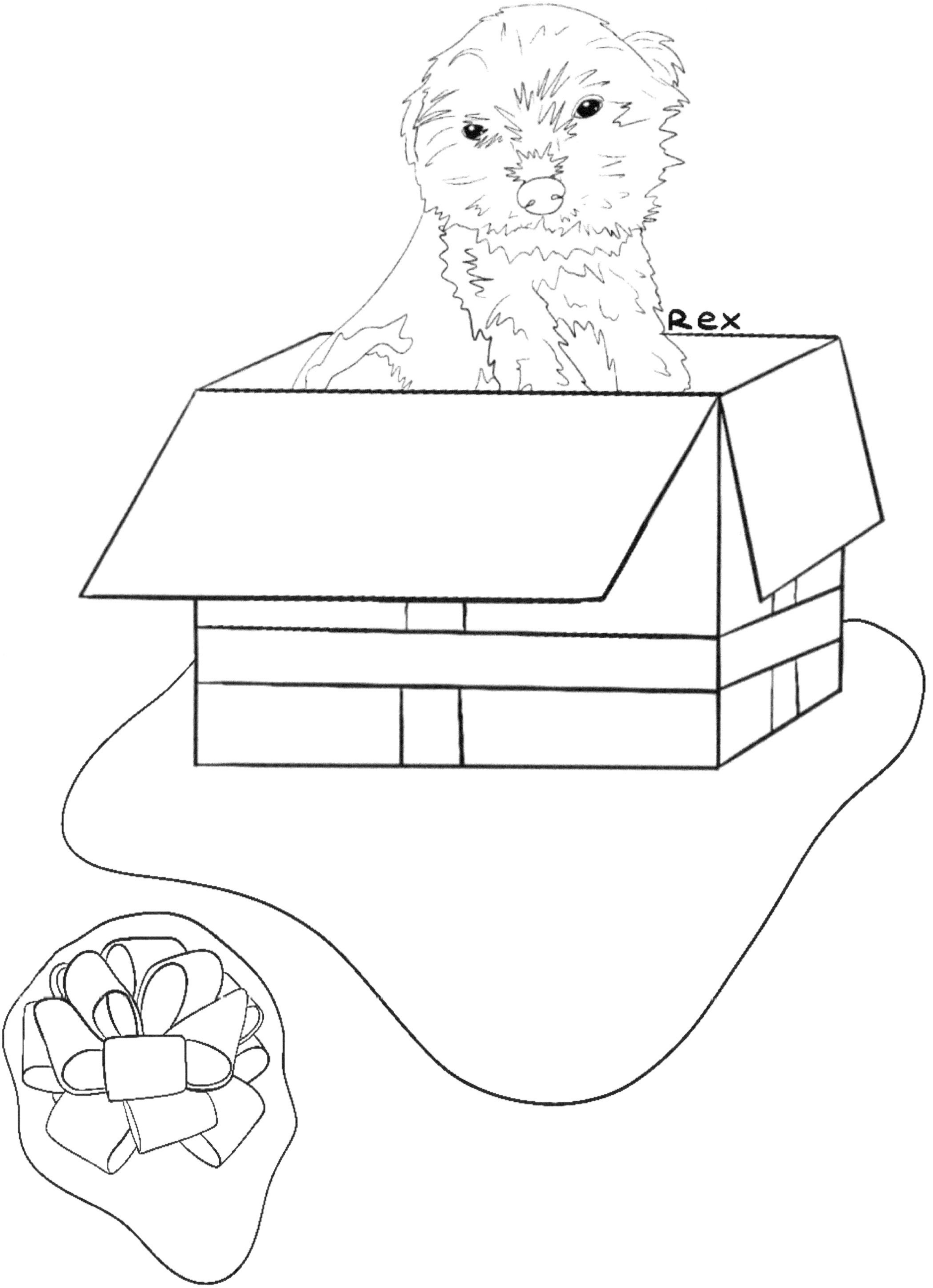
Rex

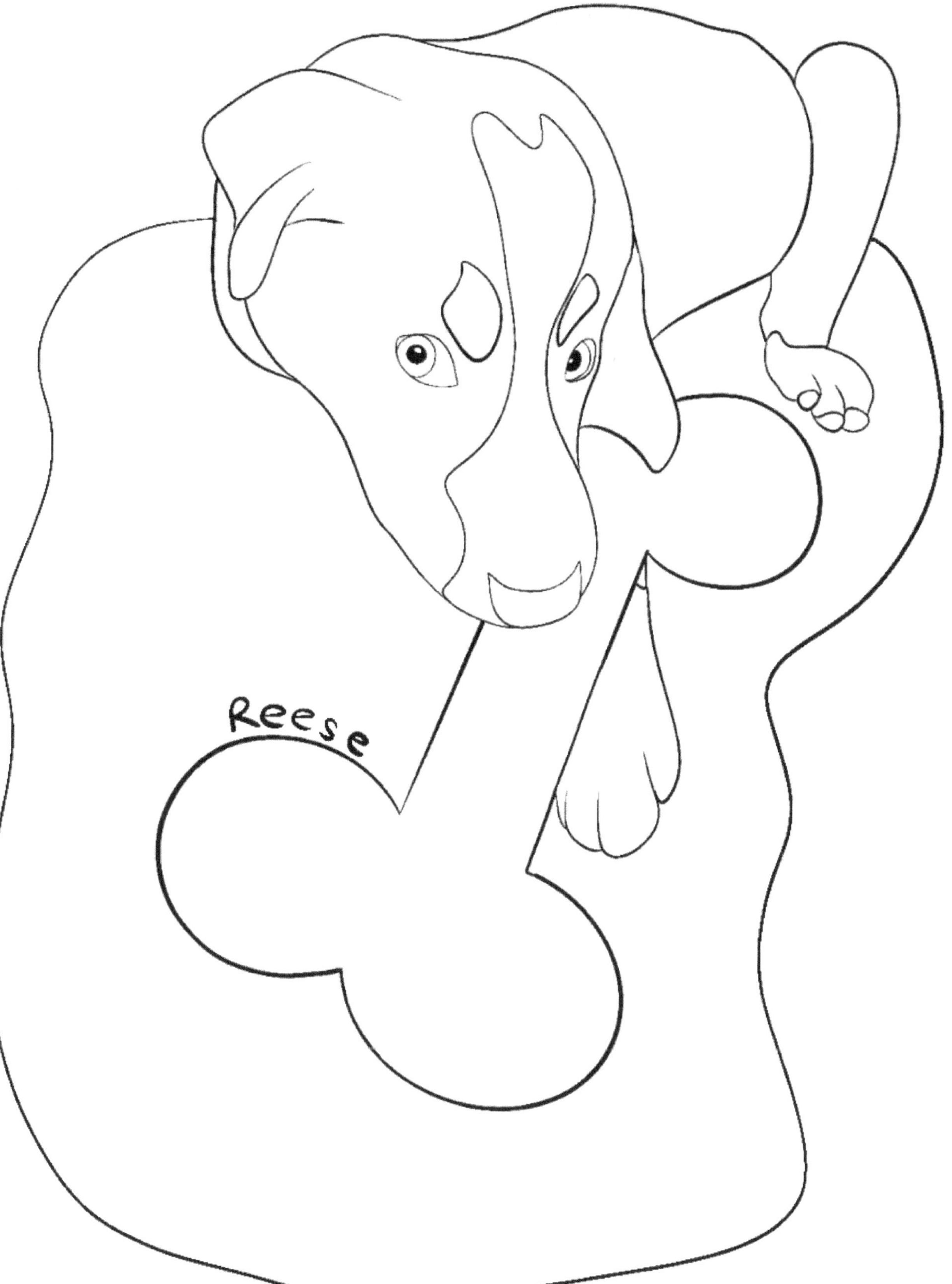
Reese

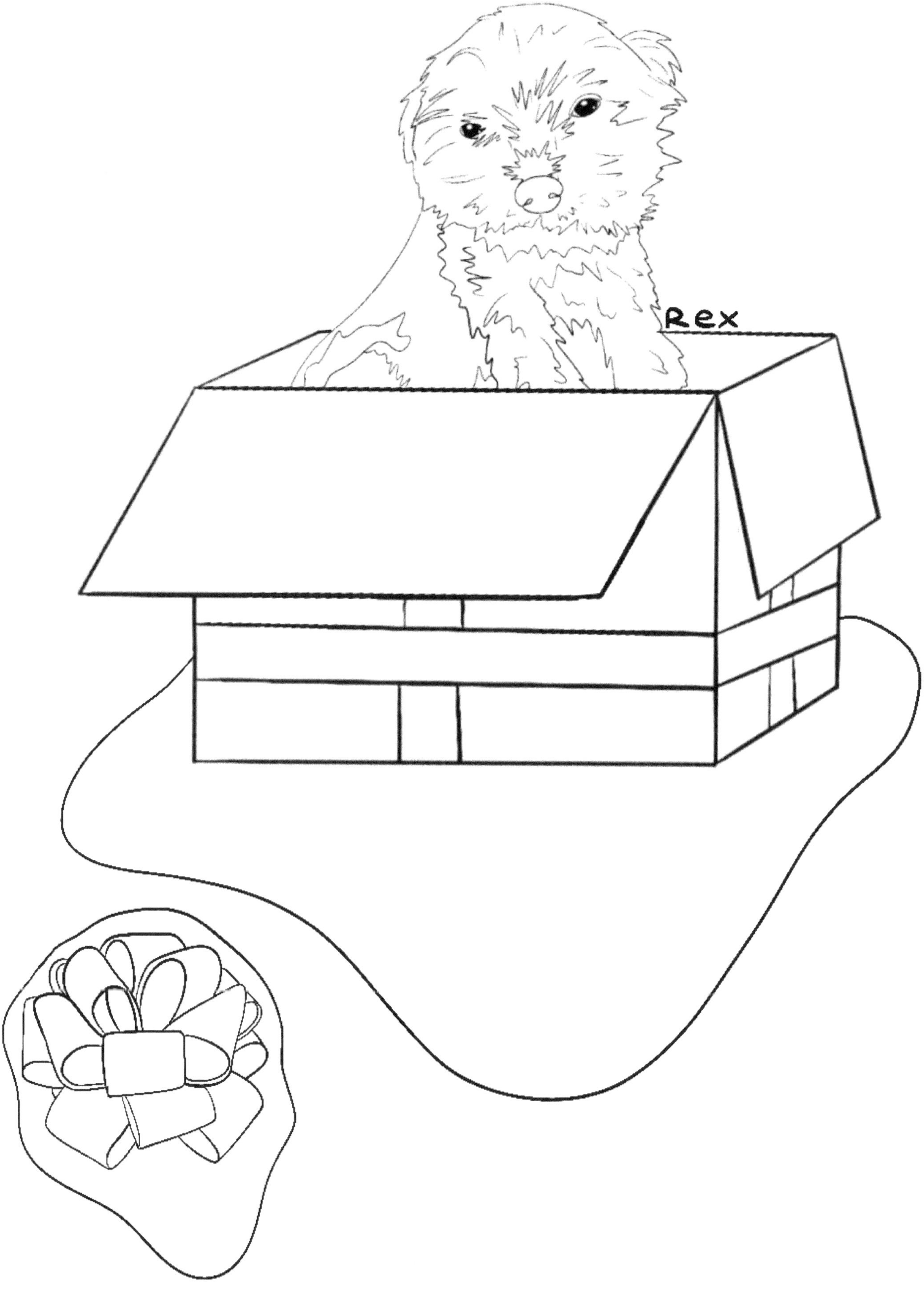
Rex

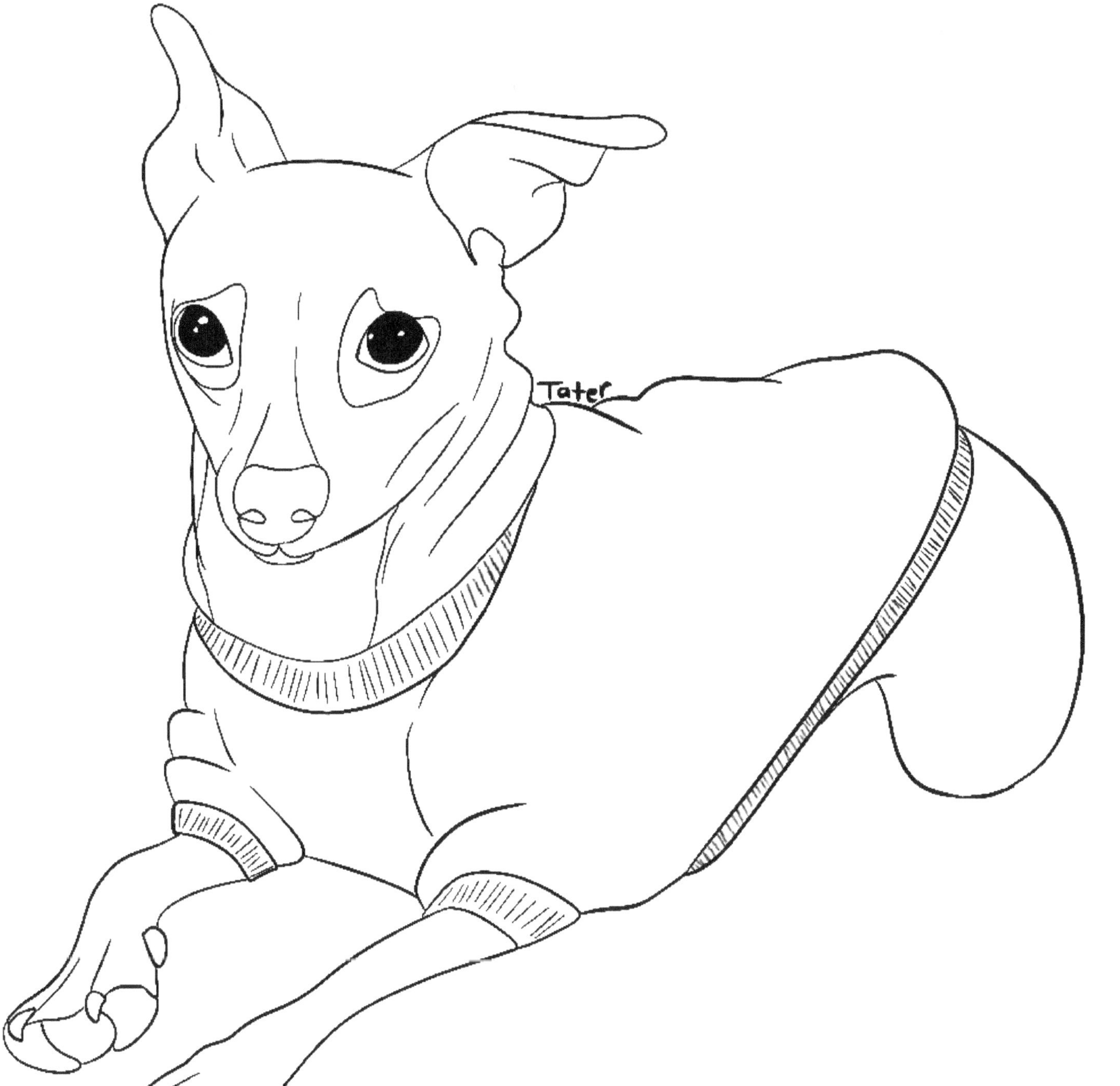
Tater

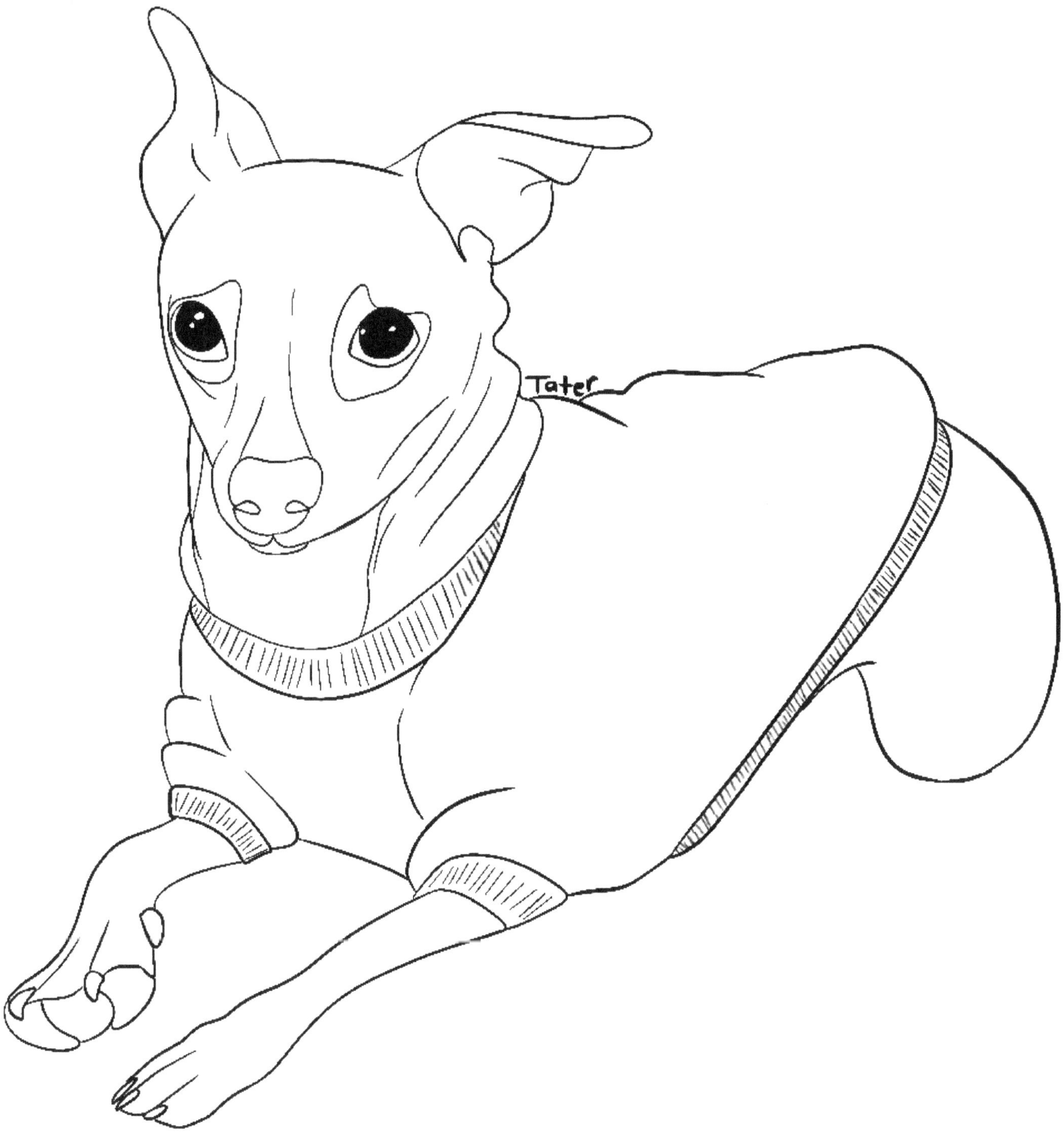
Tater

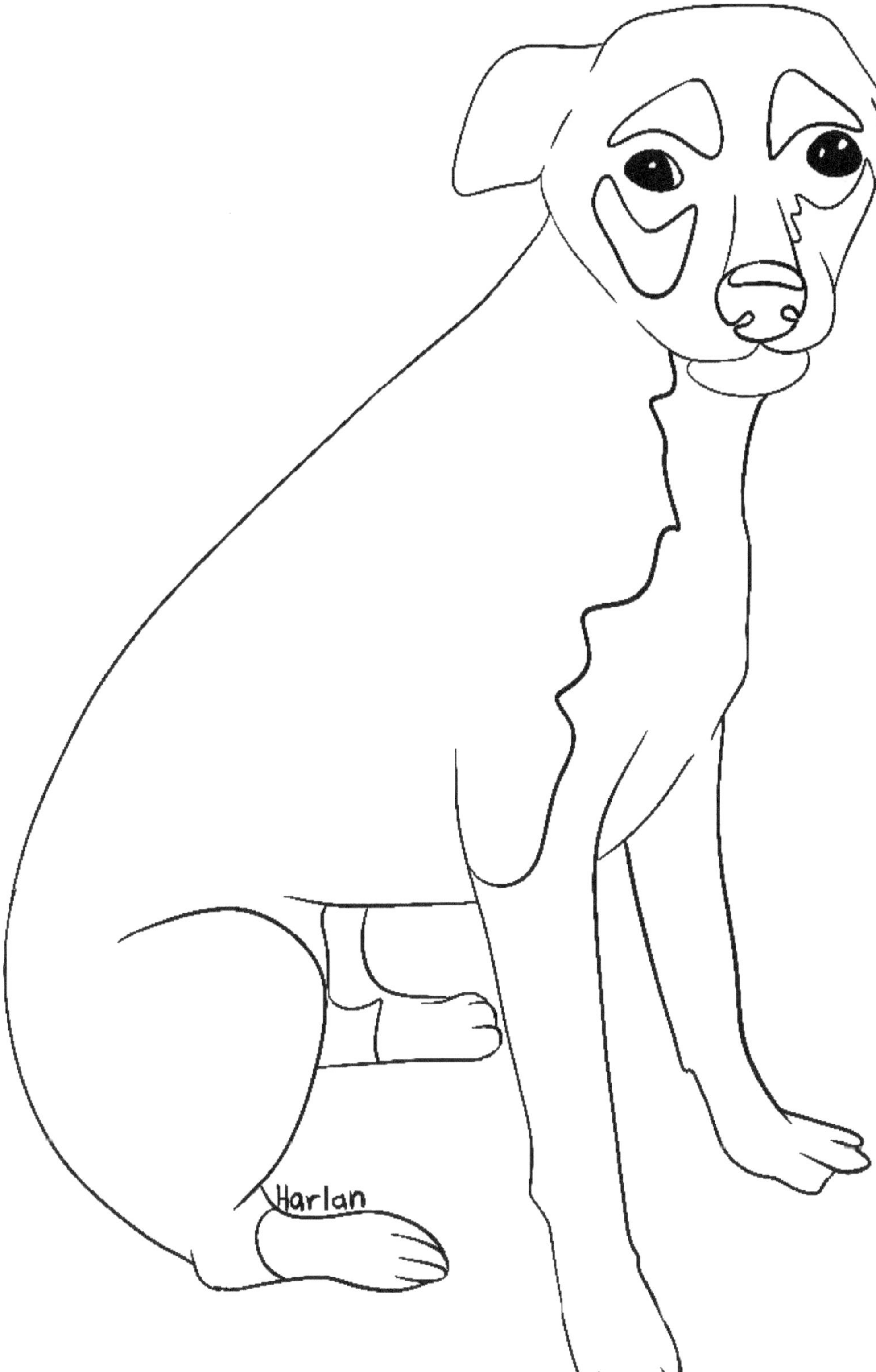
Harlan

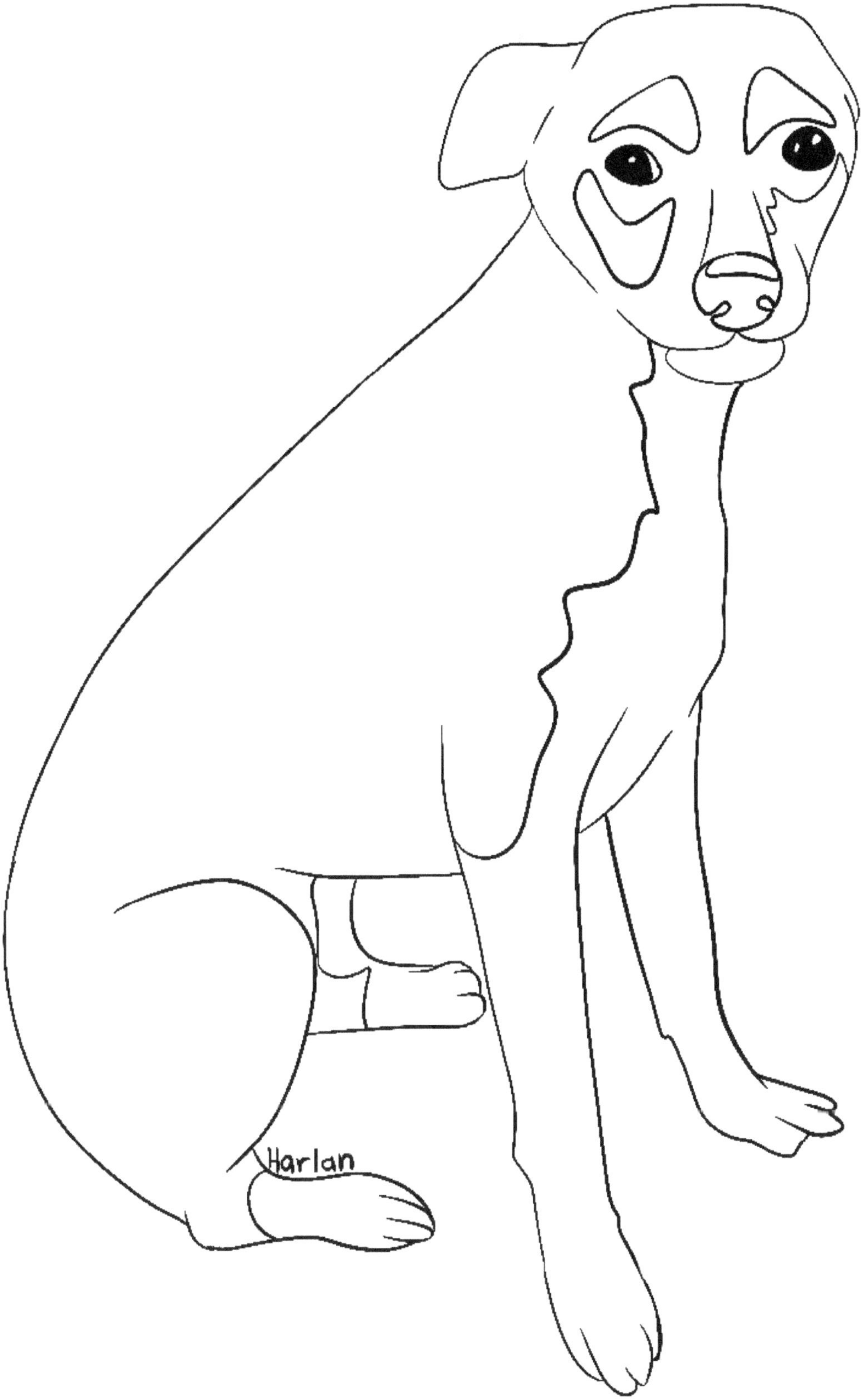
Harlan

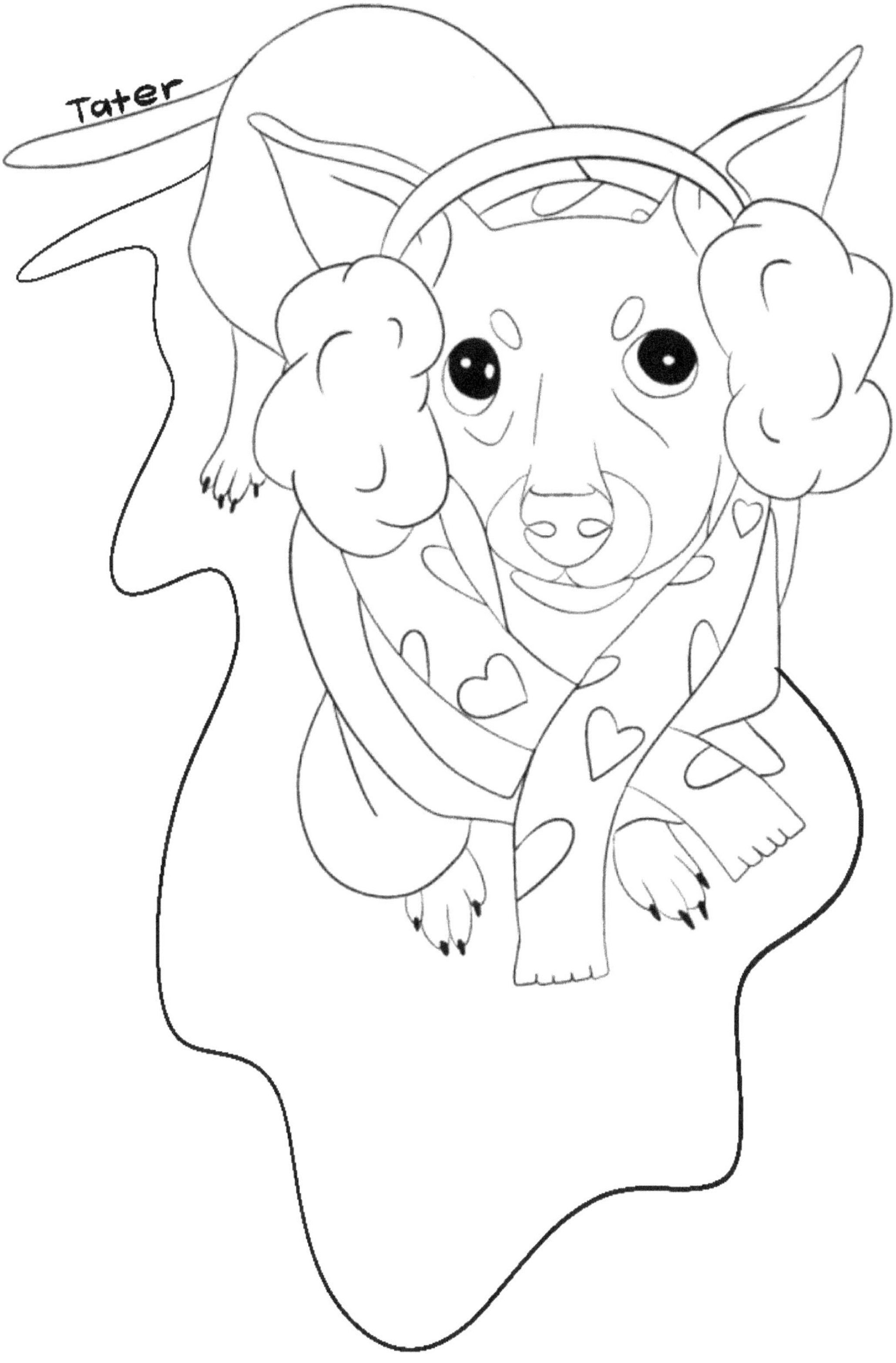
Tater

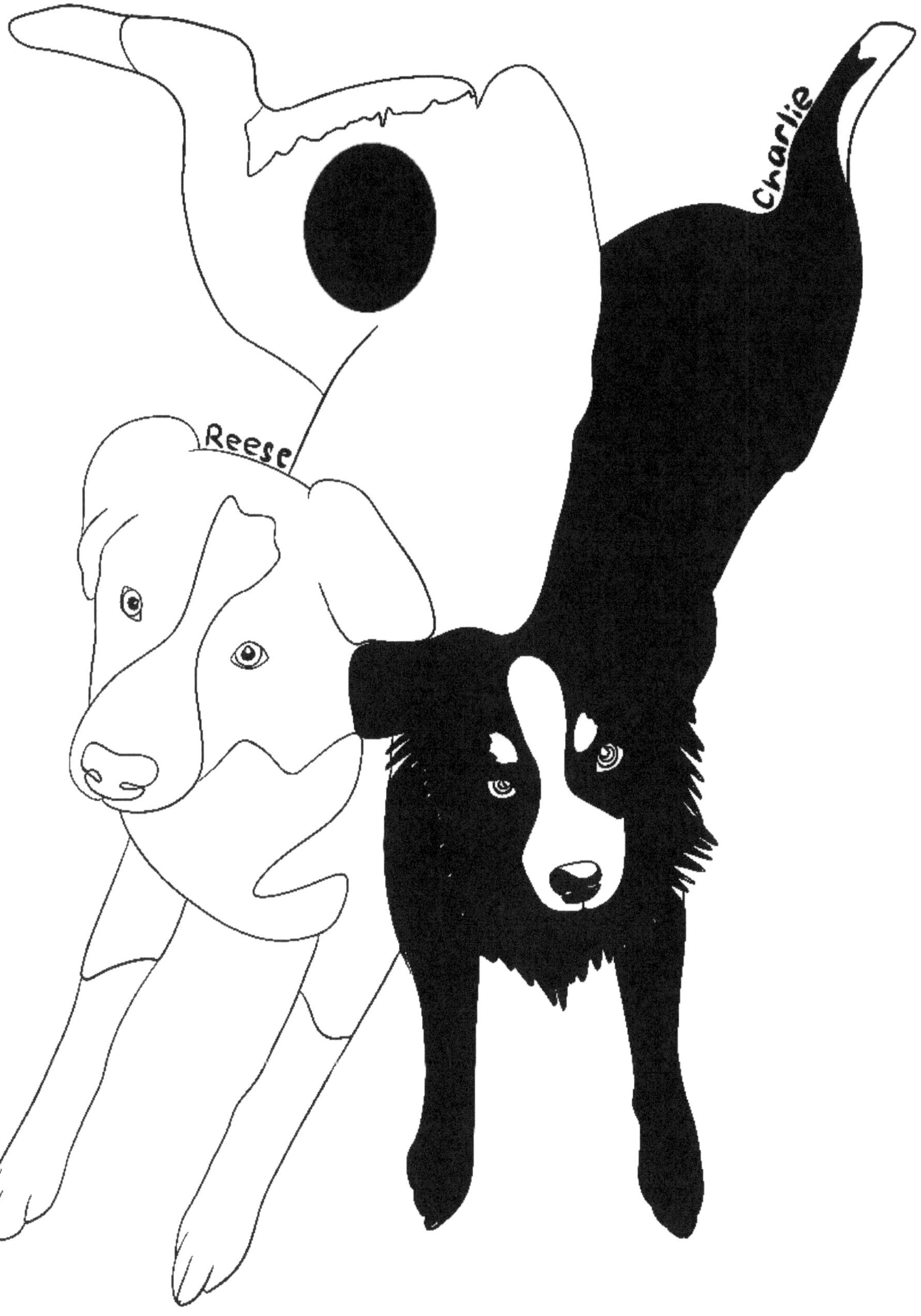
Reese
Charlie

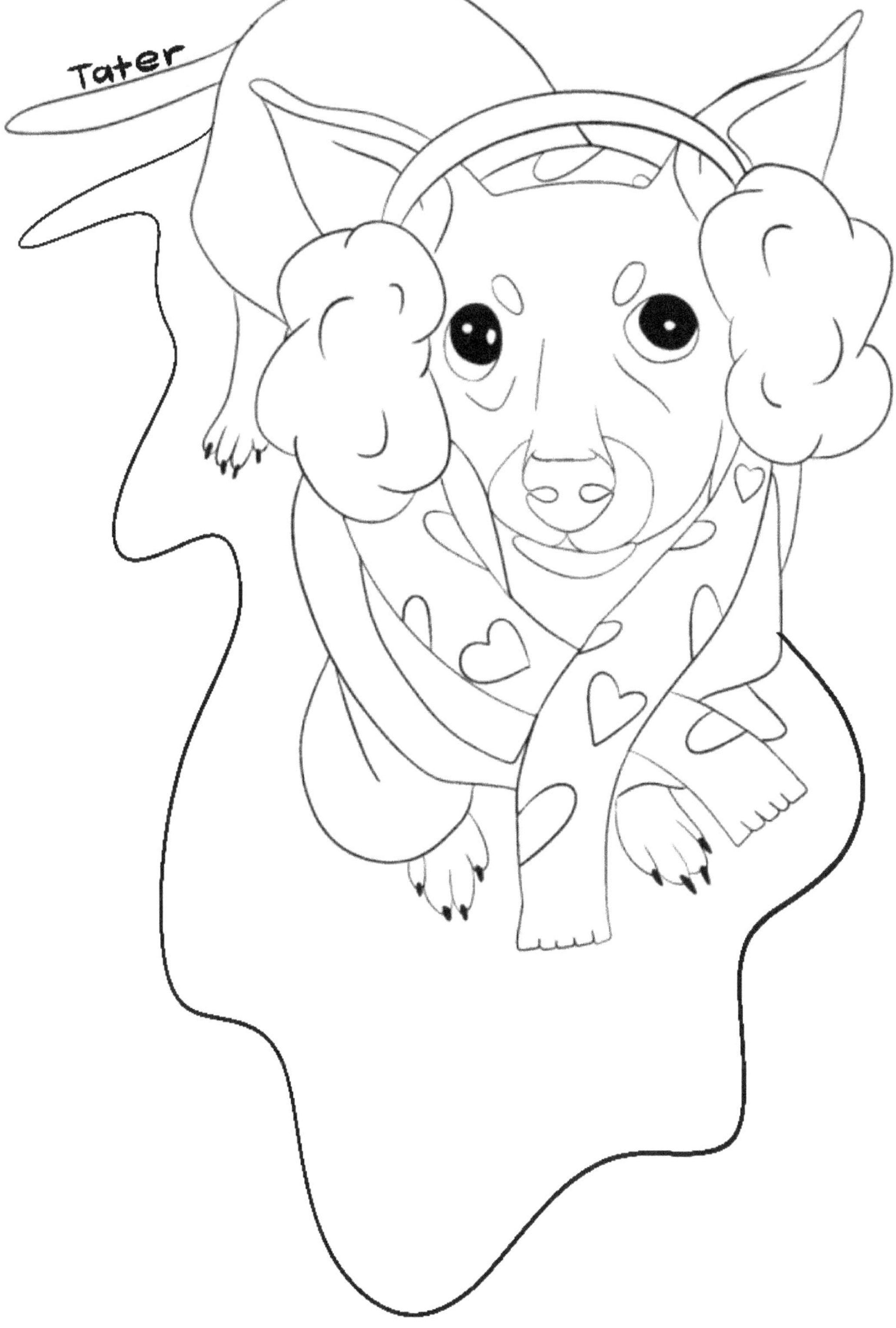
Tater

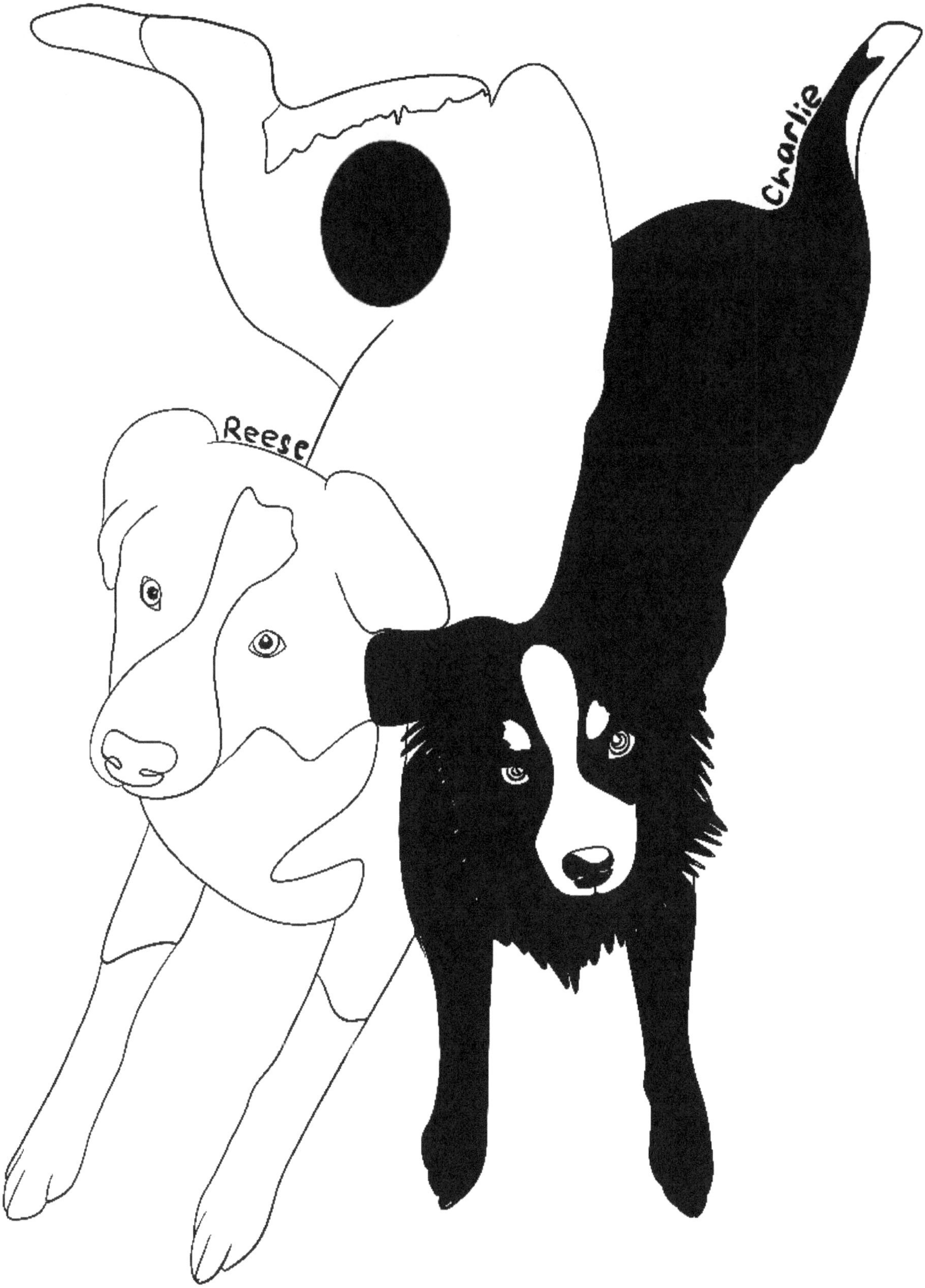
Reese
Charlie

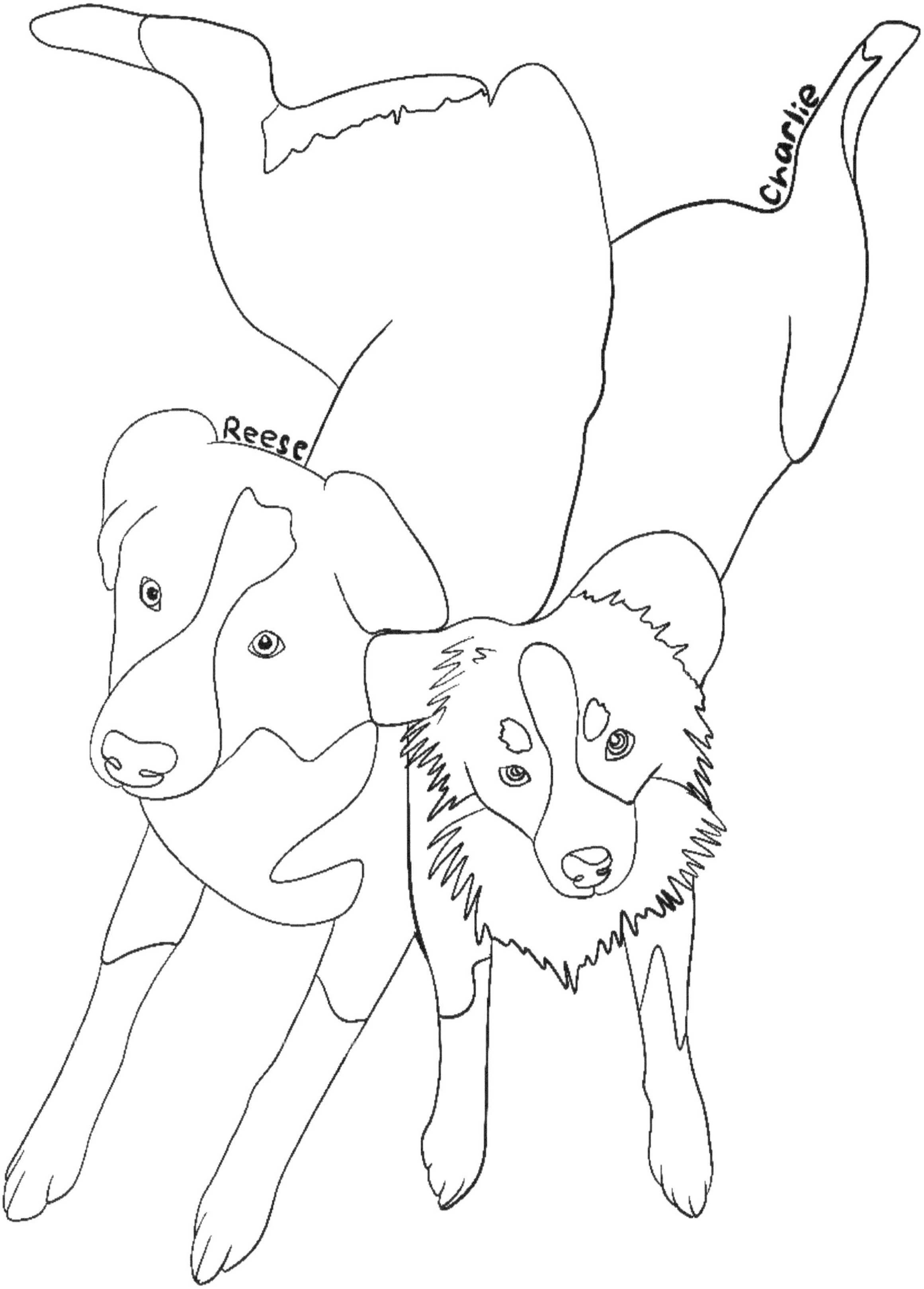
Reese
Charlie

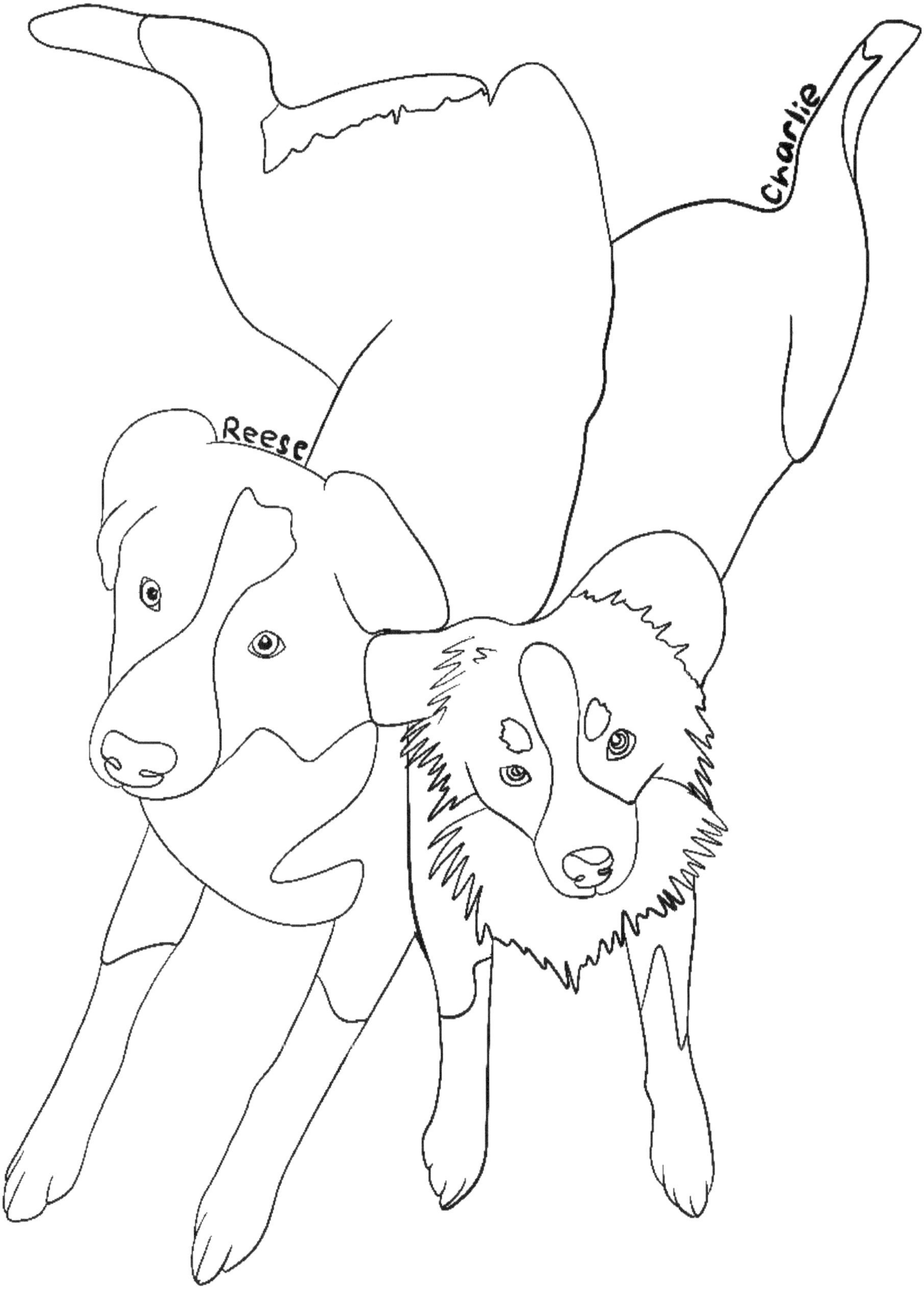
Charlie
Reese

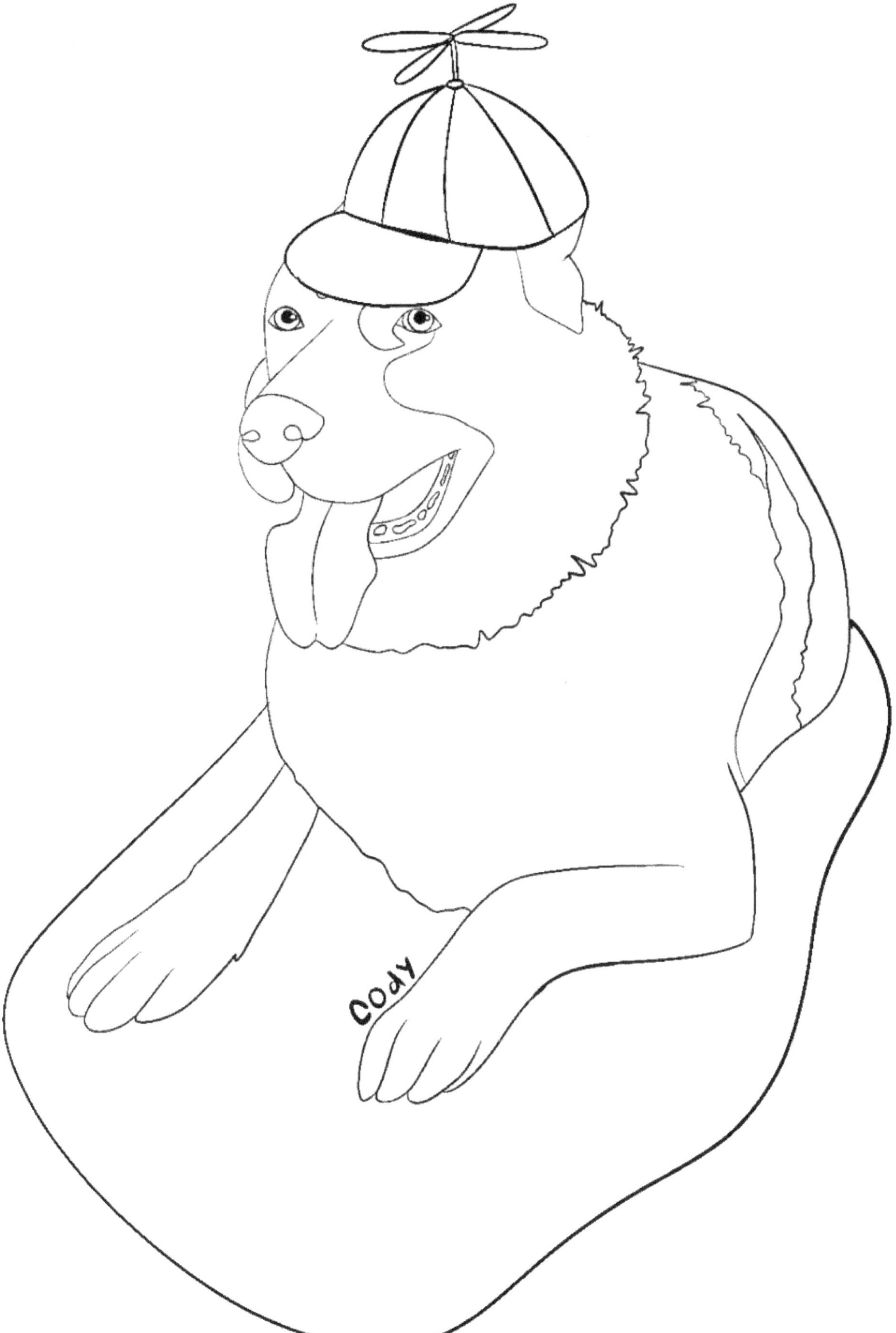
Cody

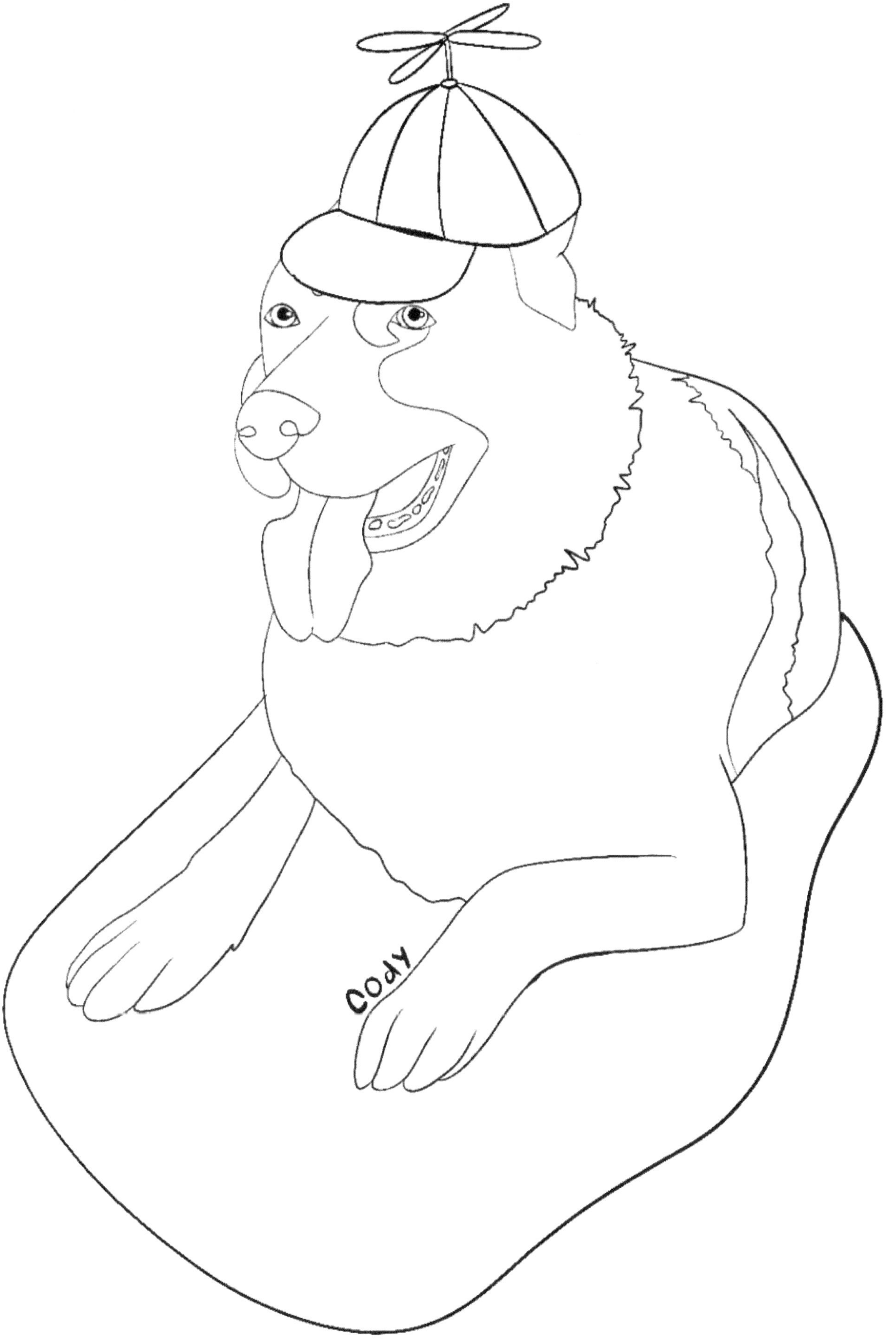
Cody

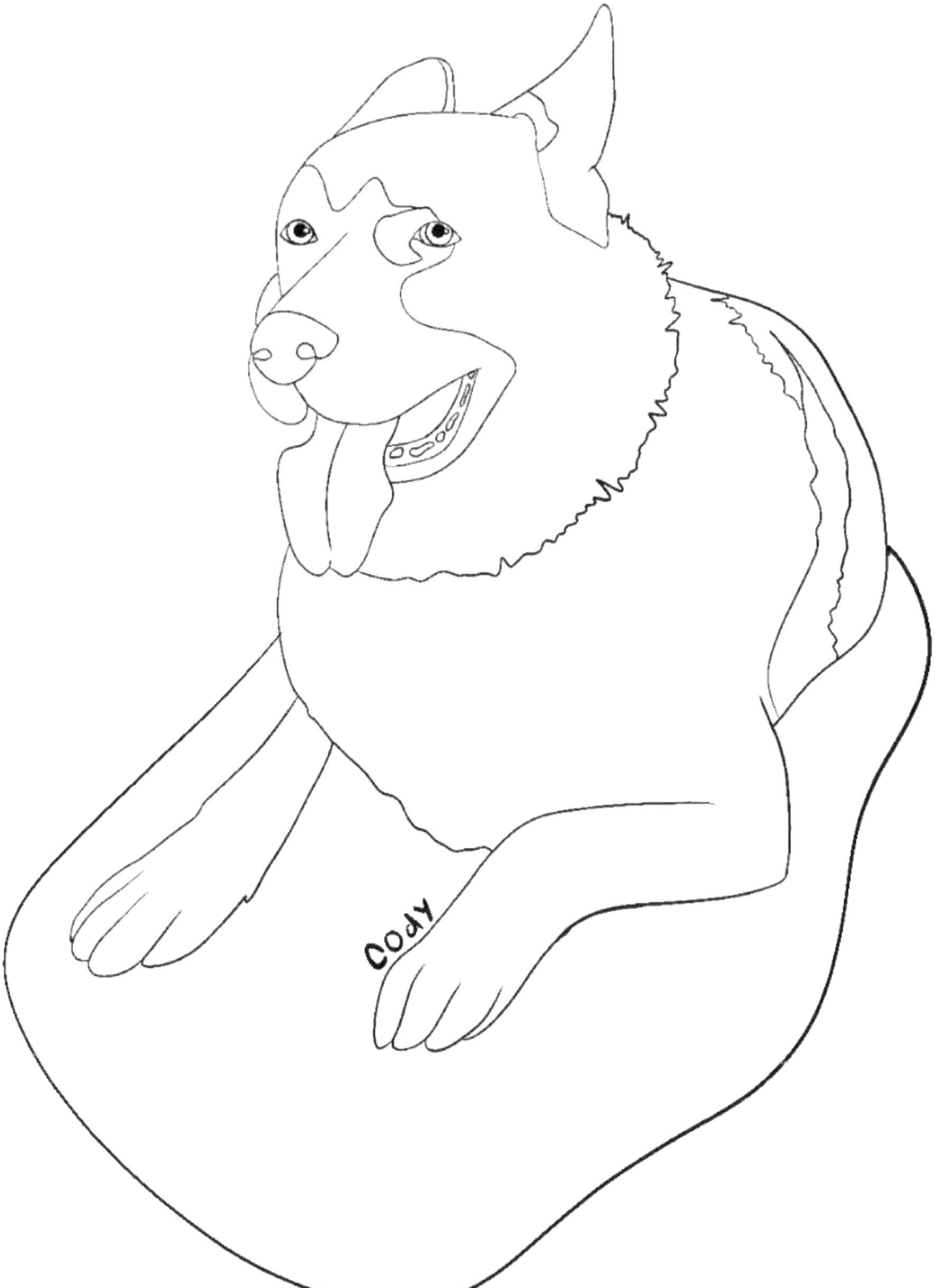
Cody

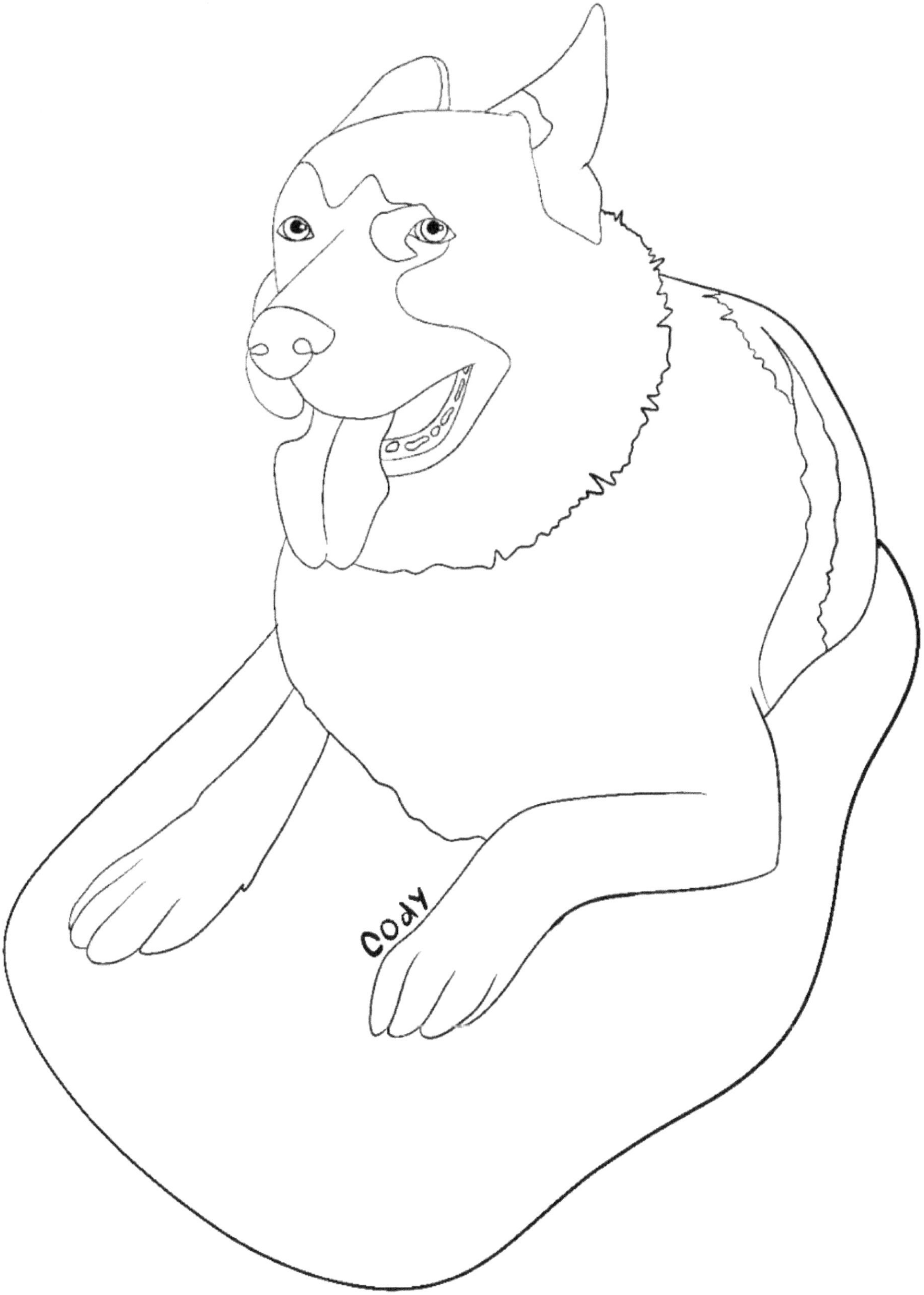
Cody

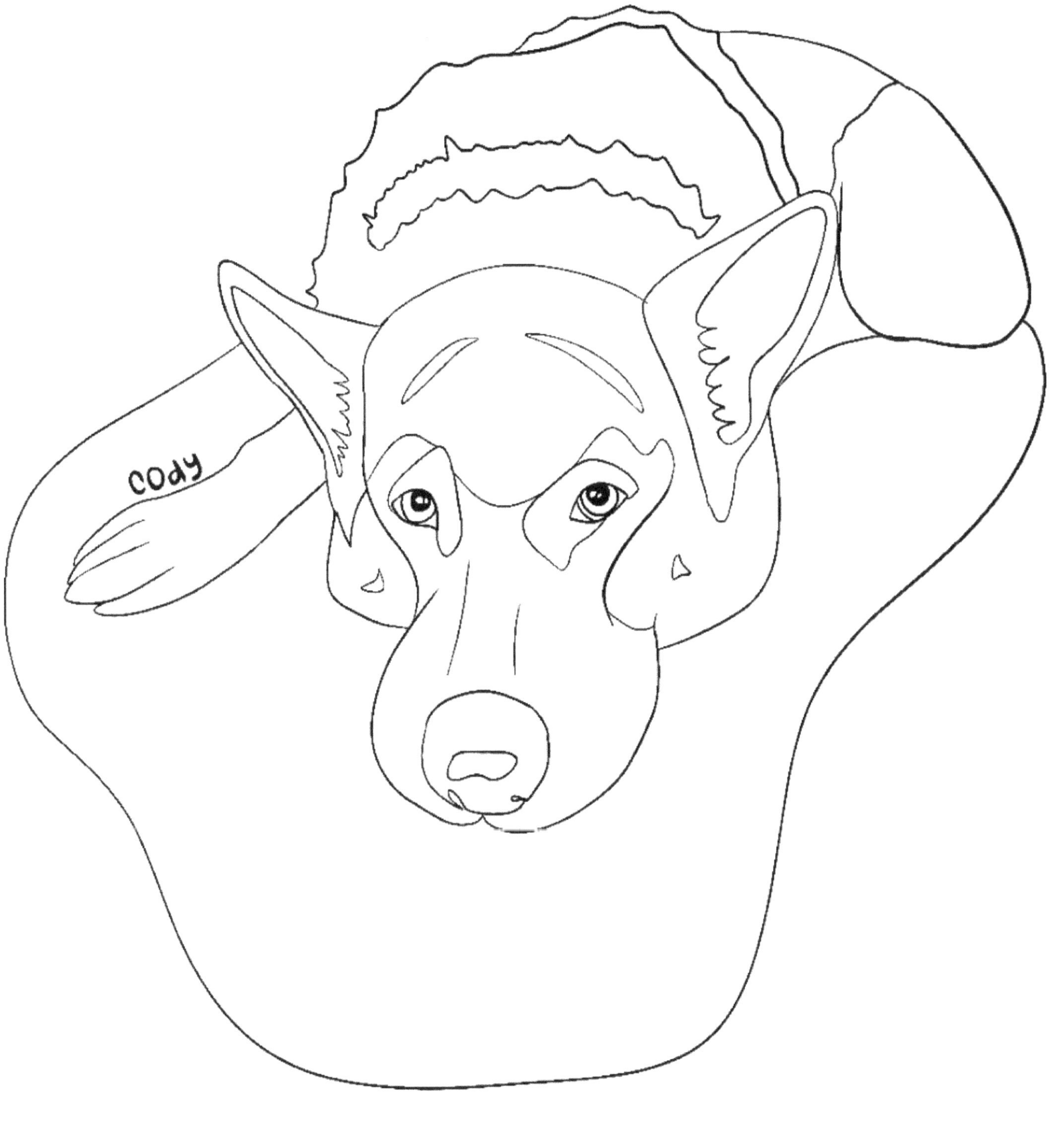
cody

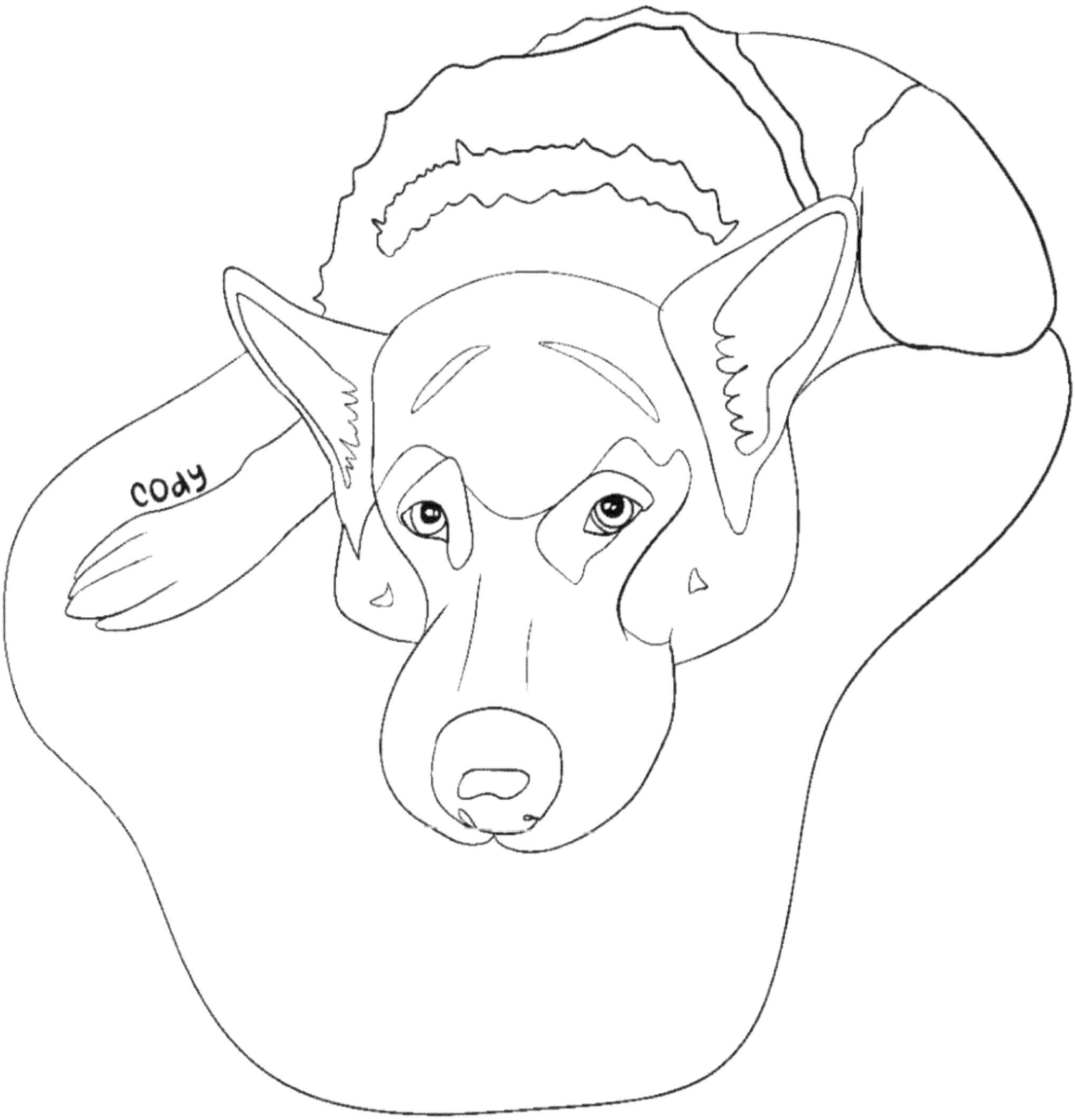
Cody

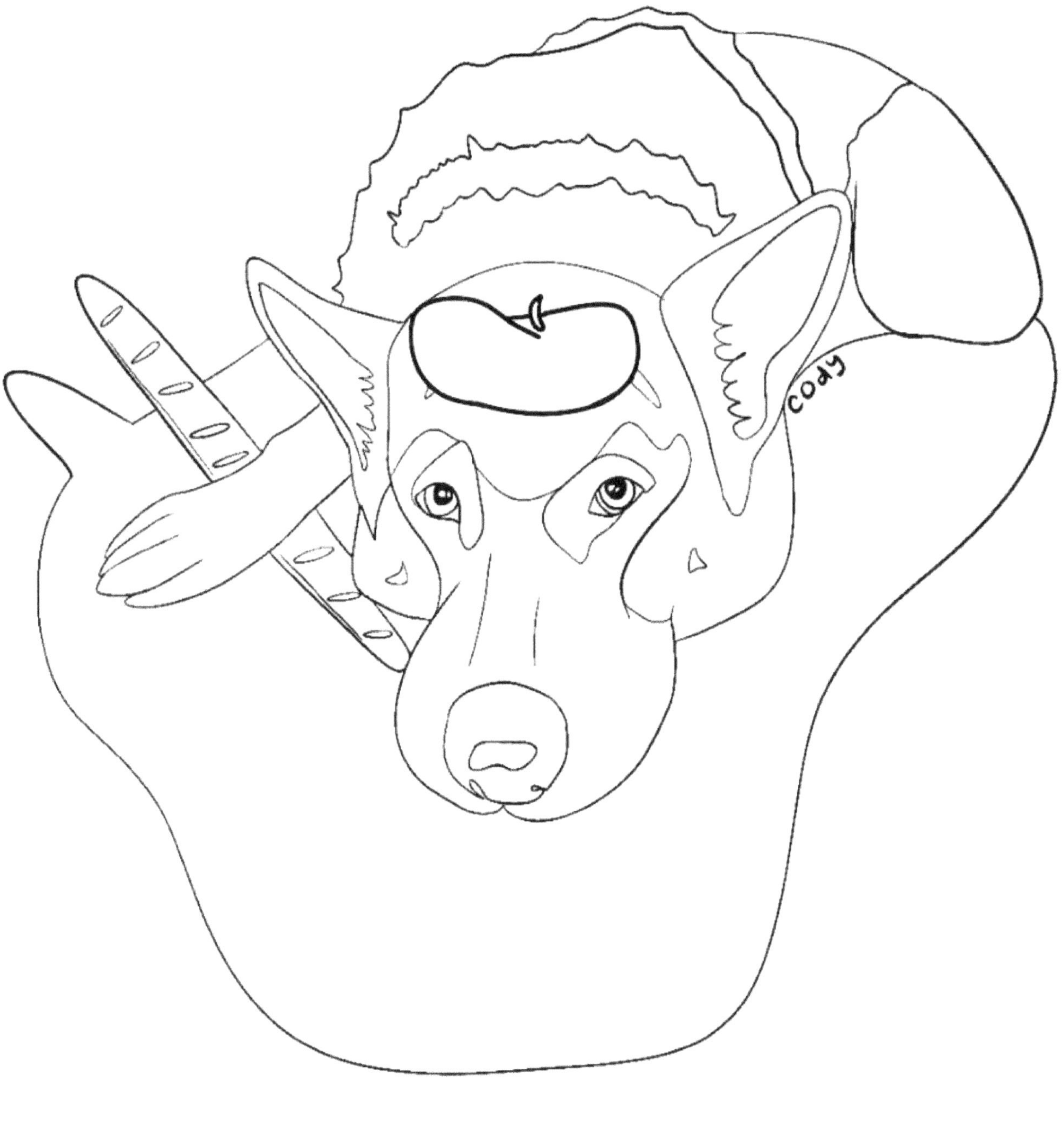
cody

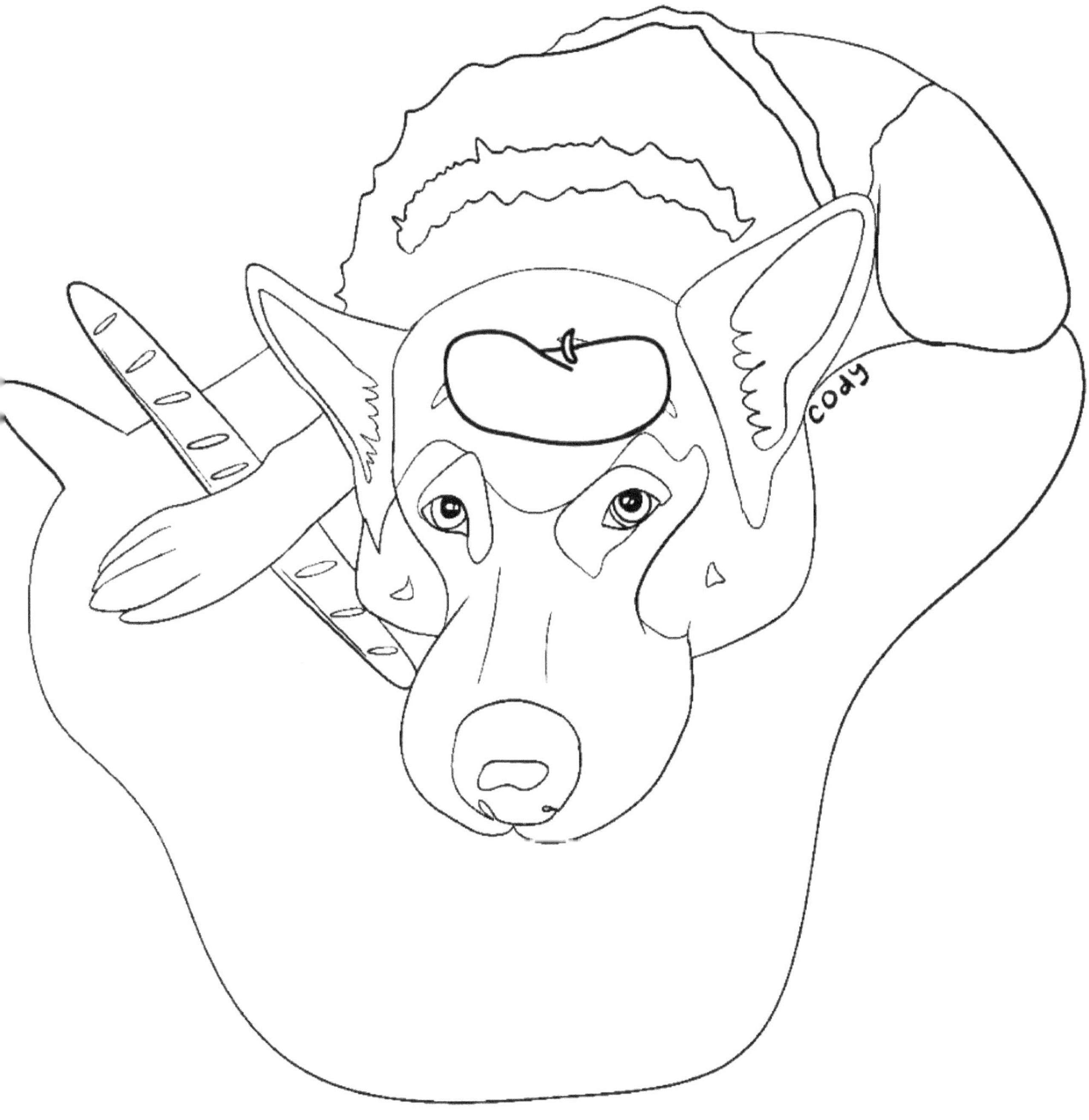
cody

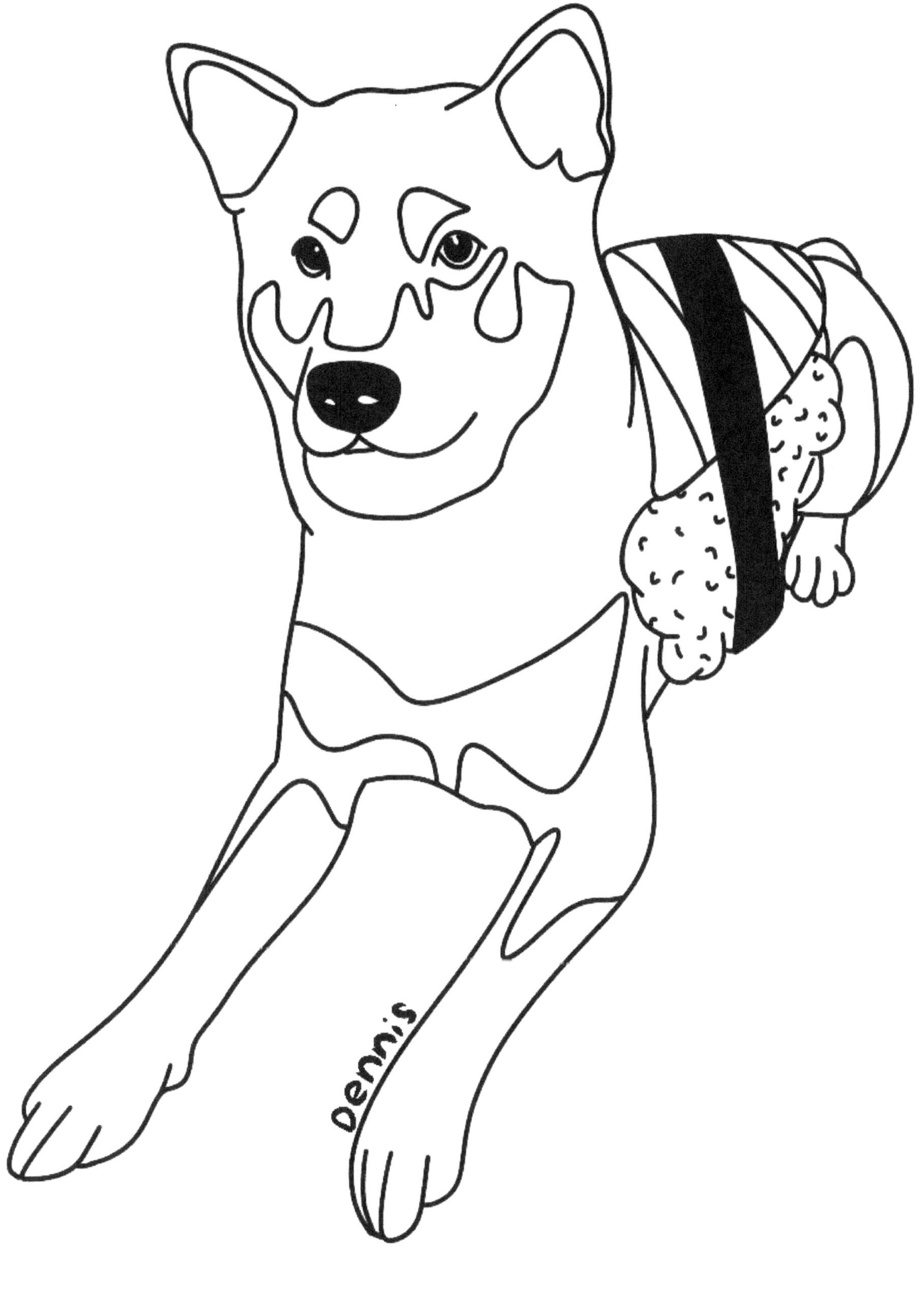
Dennis

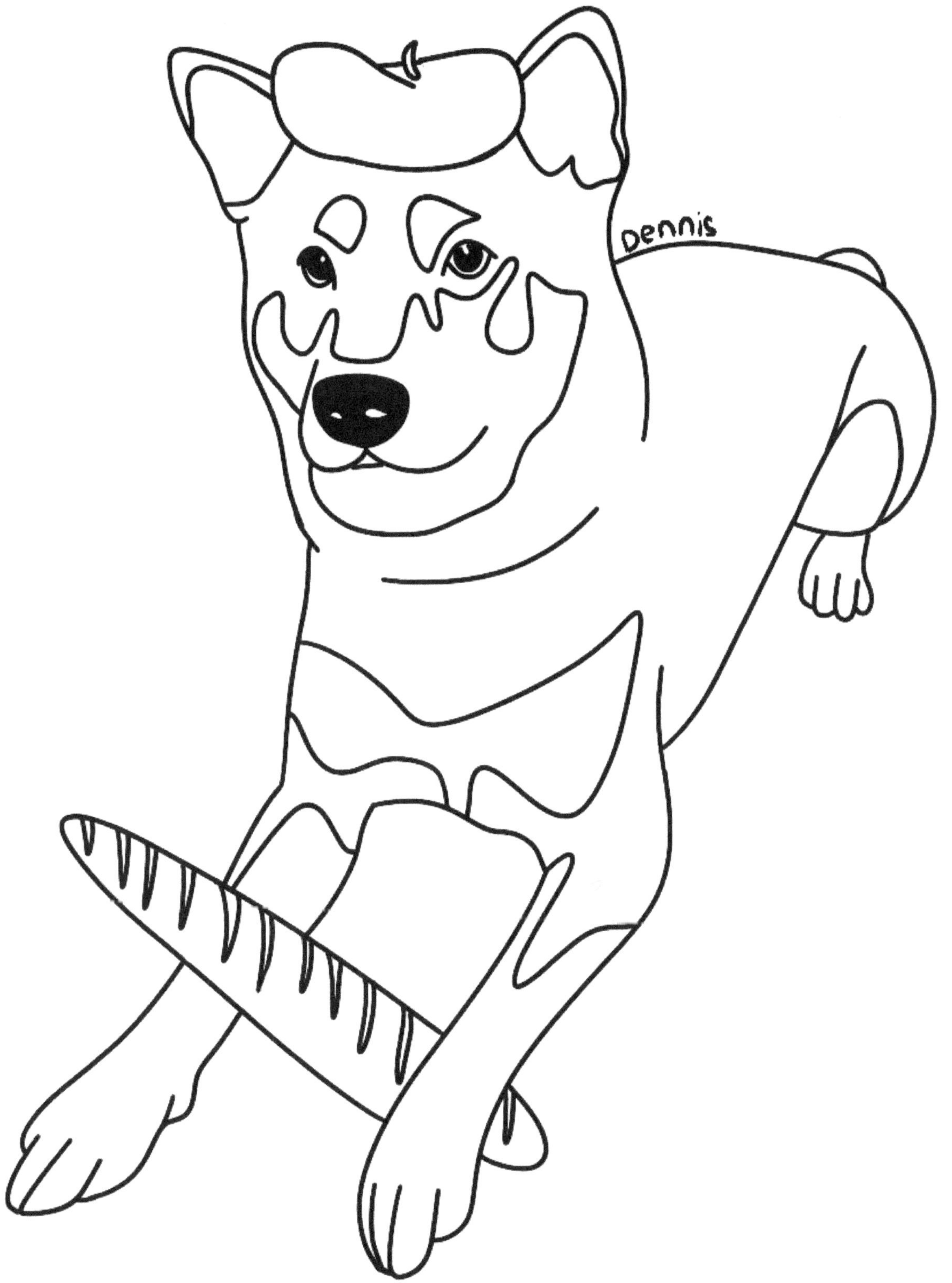
Dennis

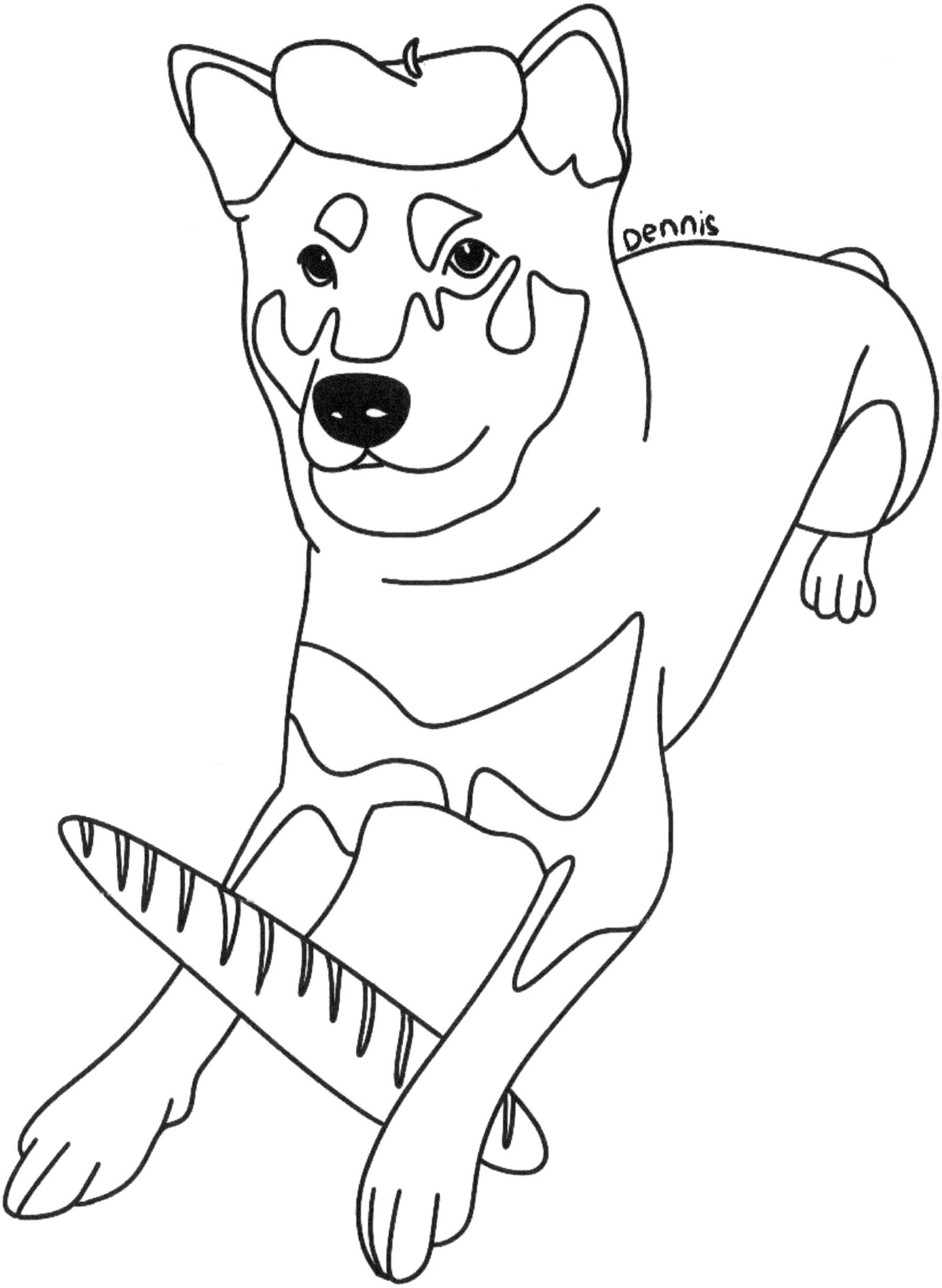
Dennis

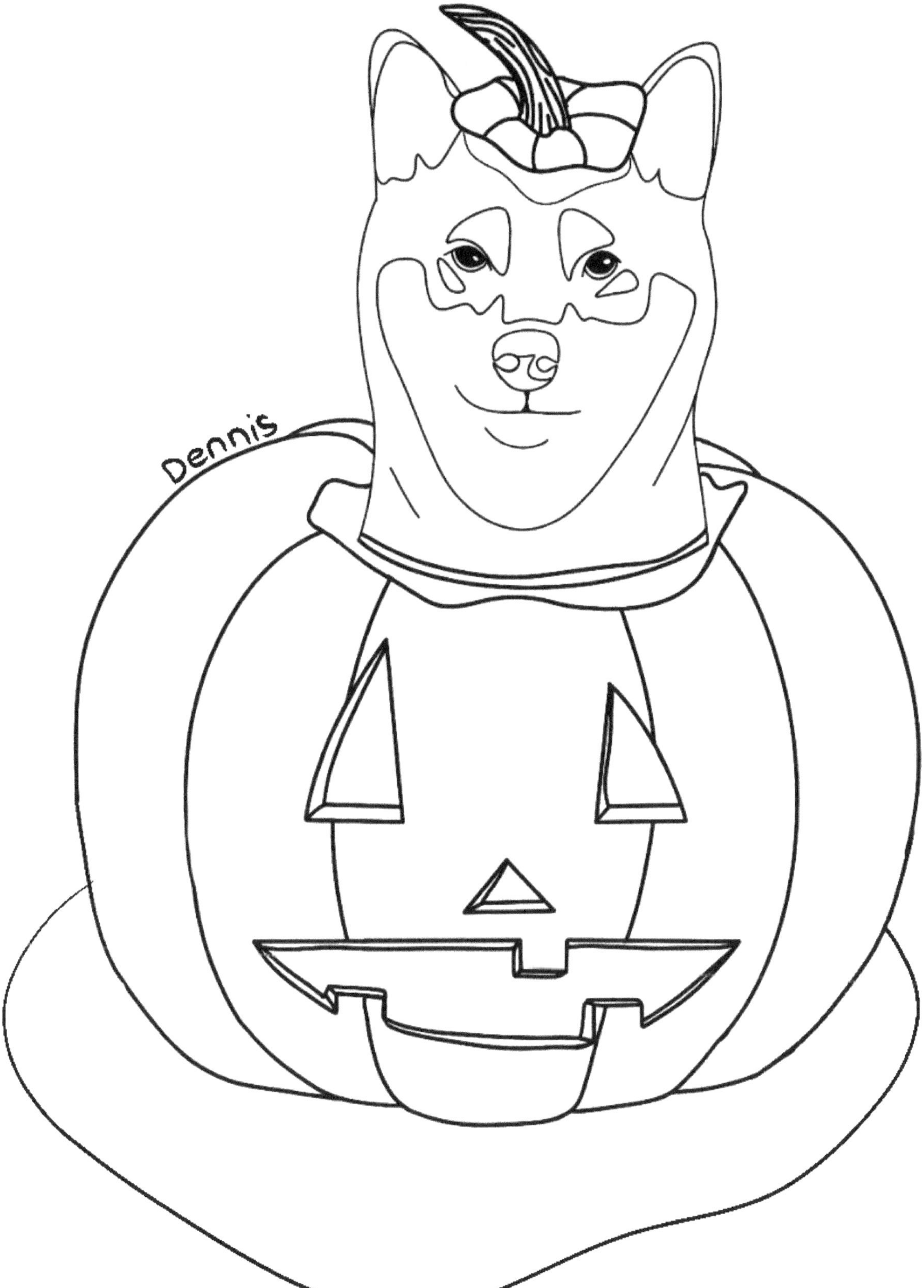
Dennis

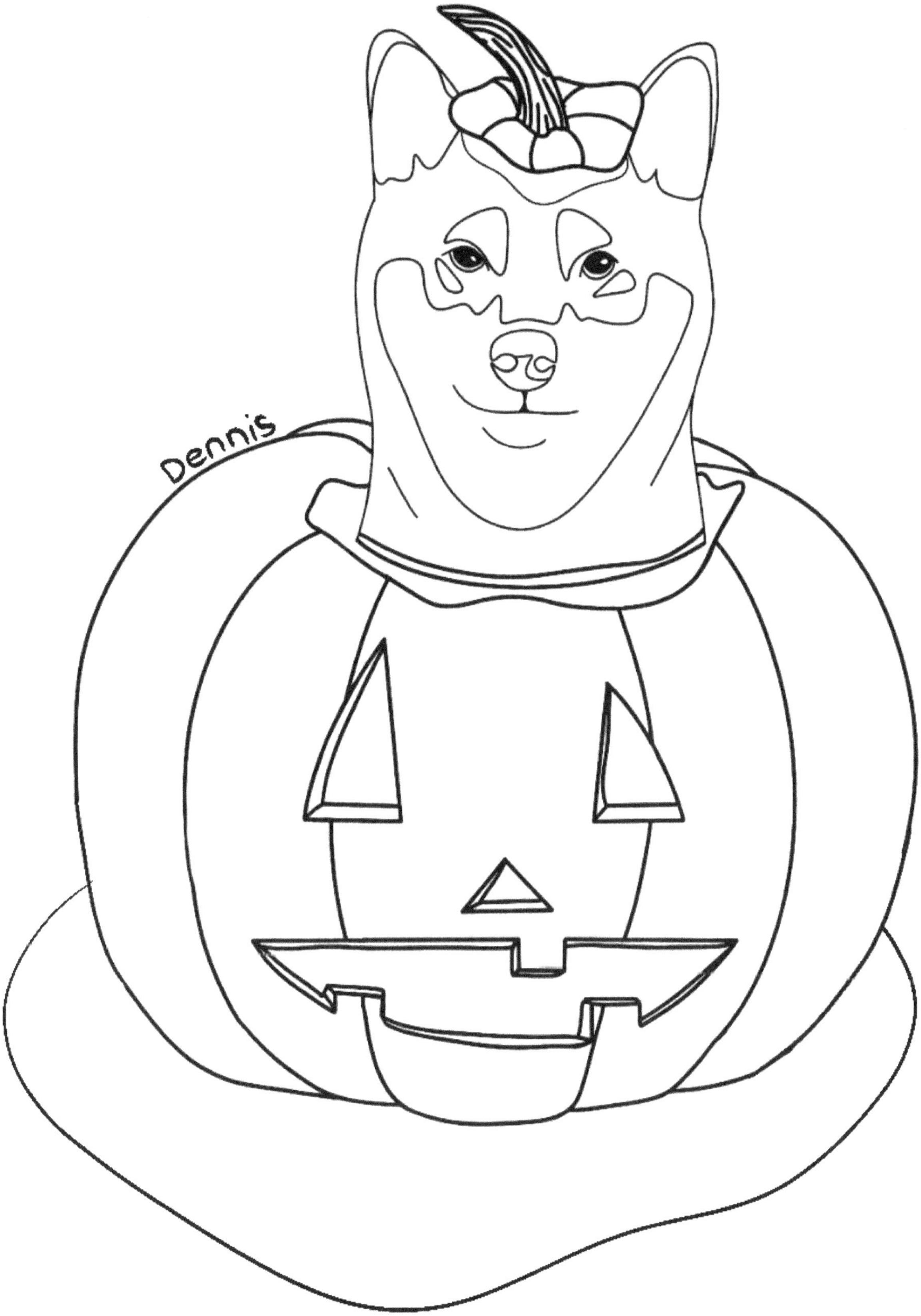
Dennis

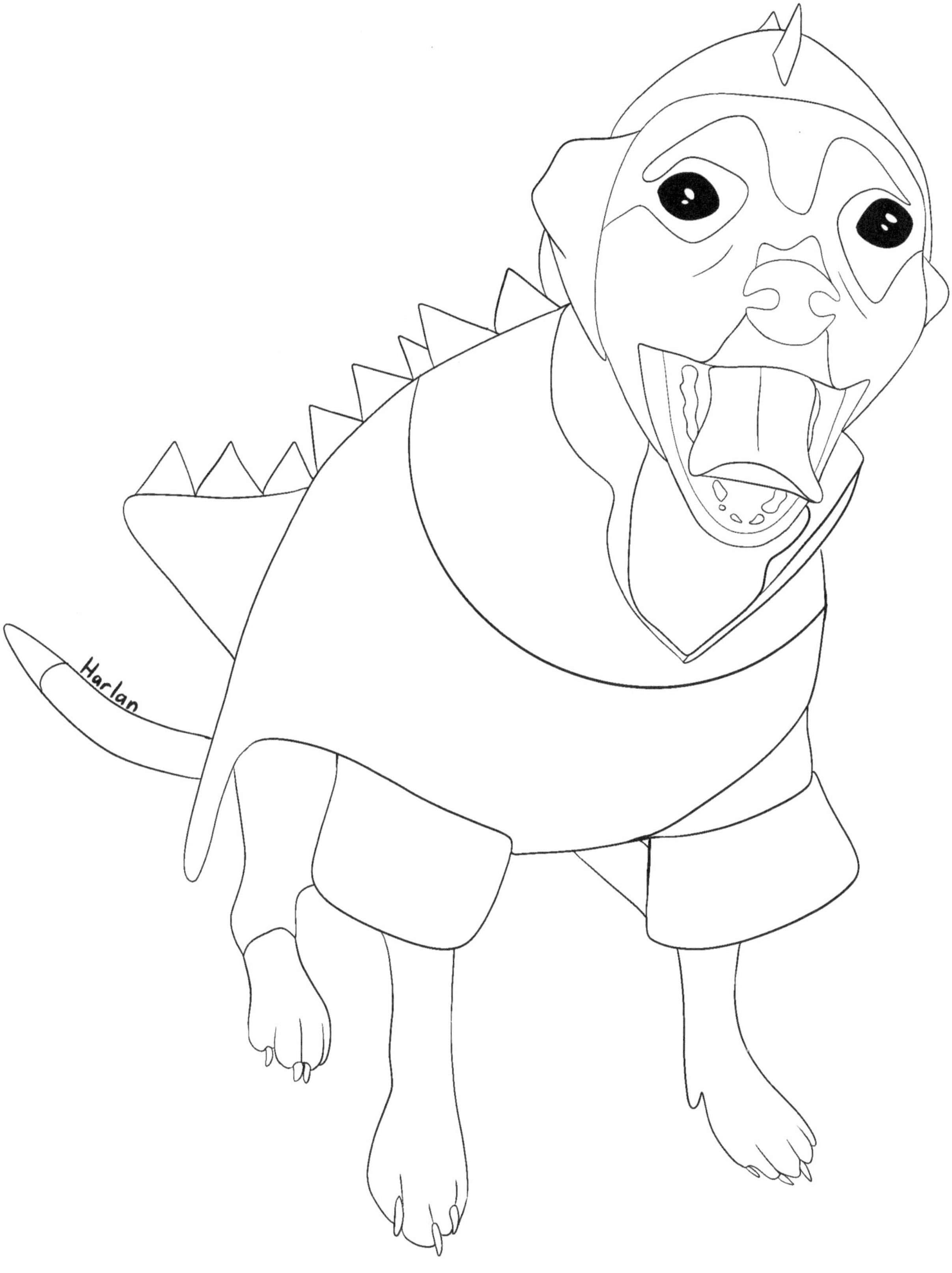
Harlan

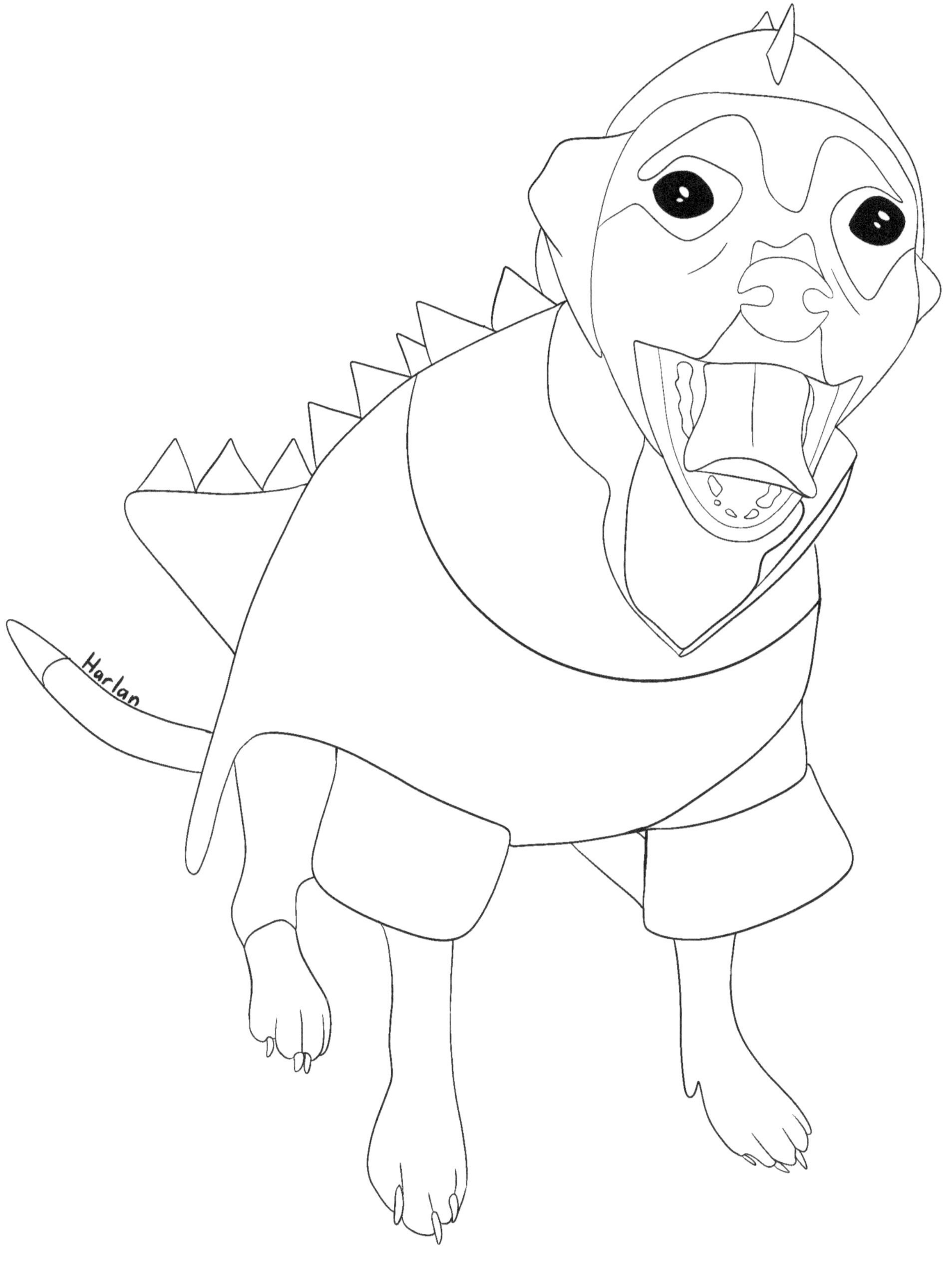
Harlan

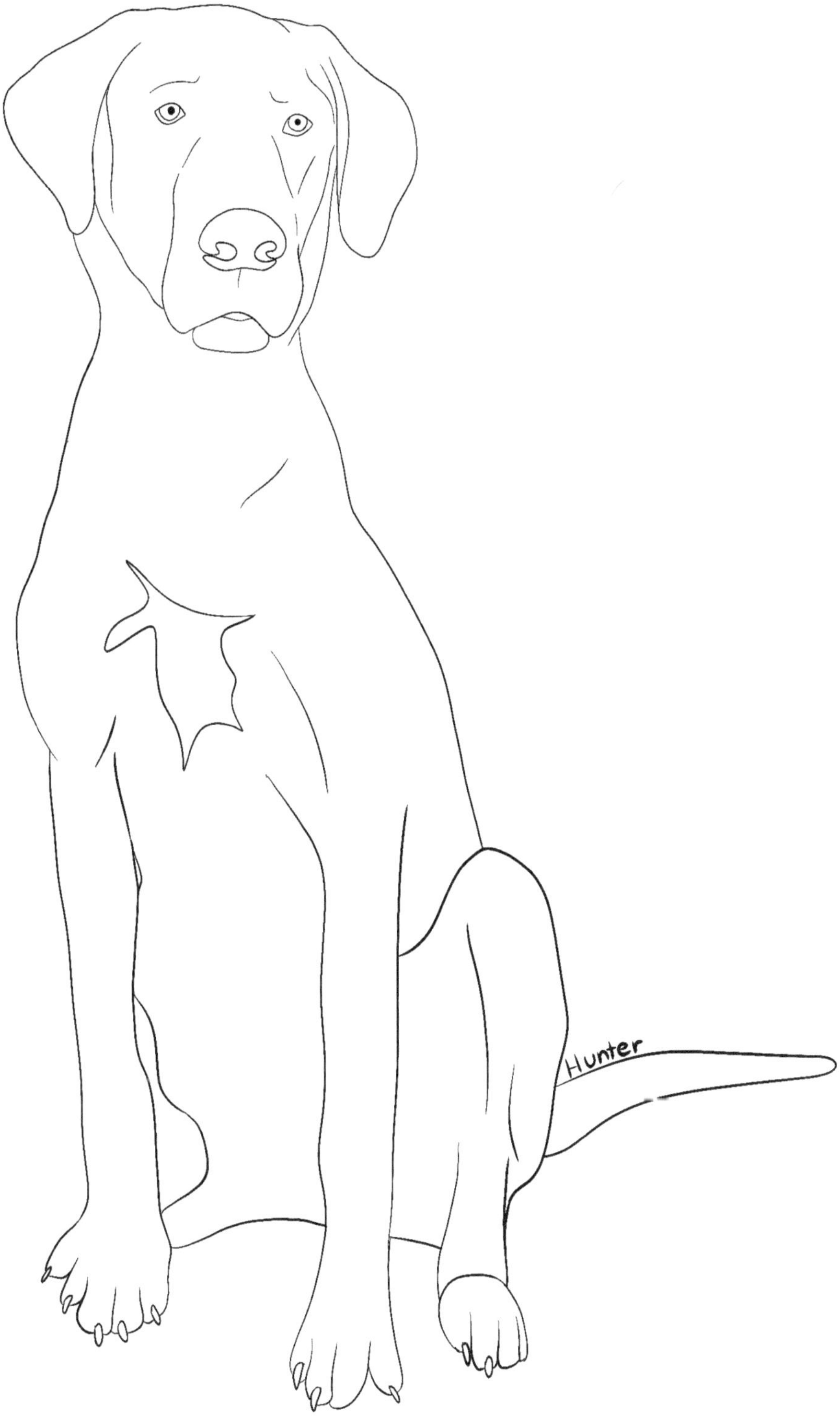
Hunter

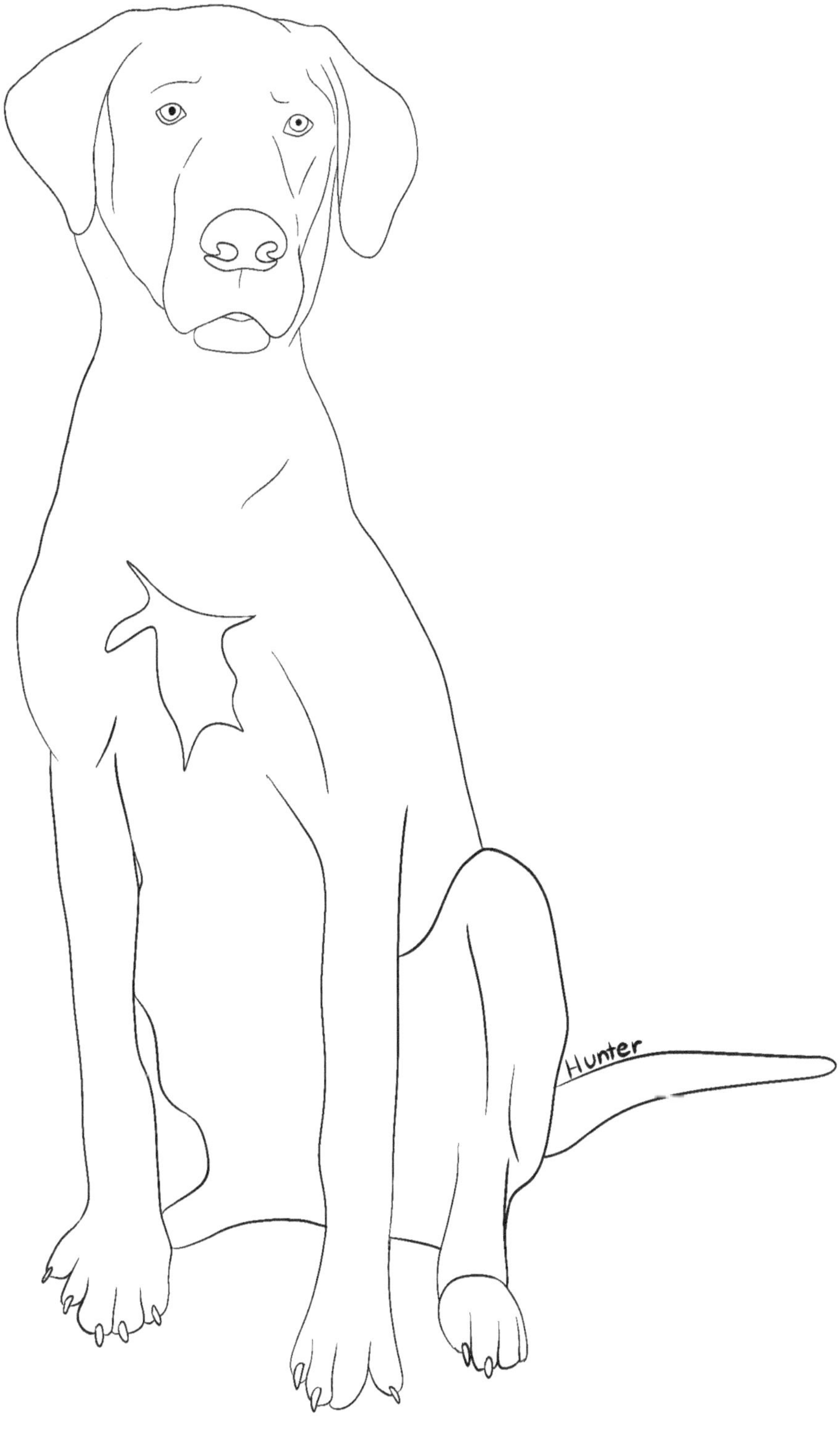
Hunter

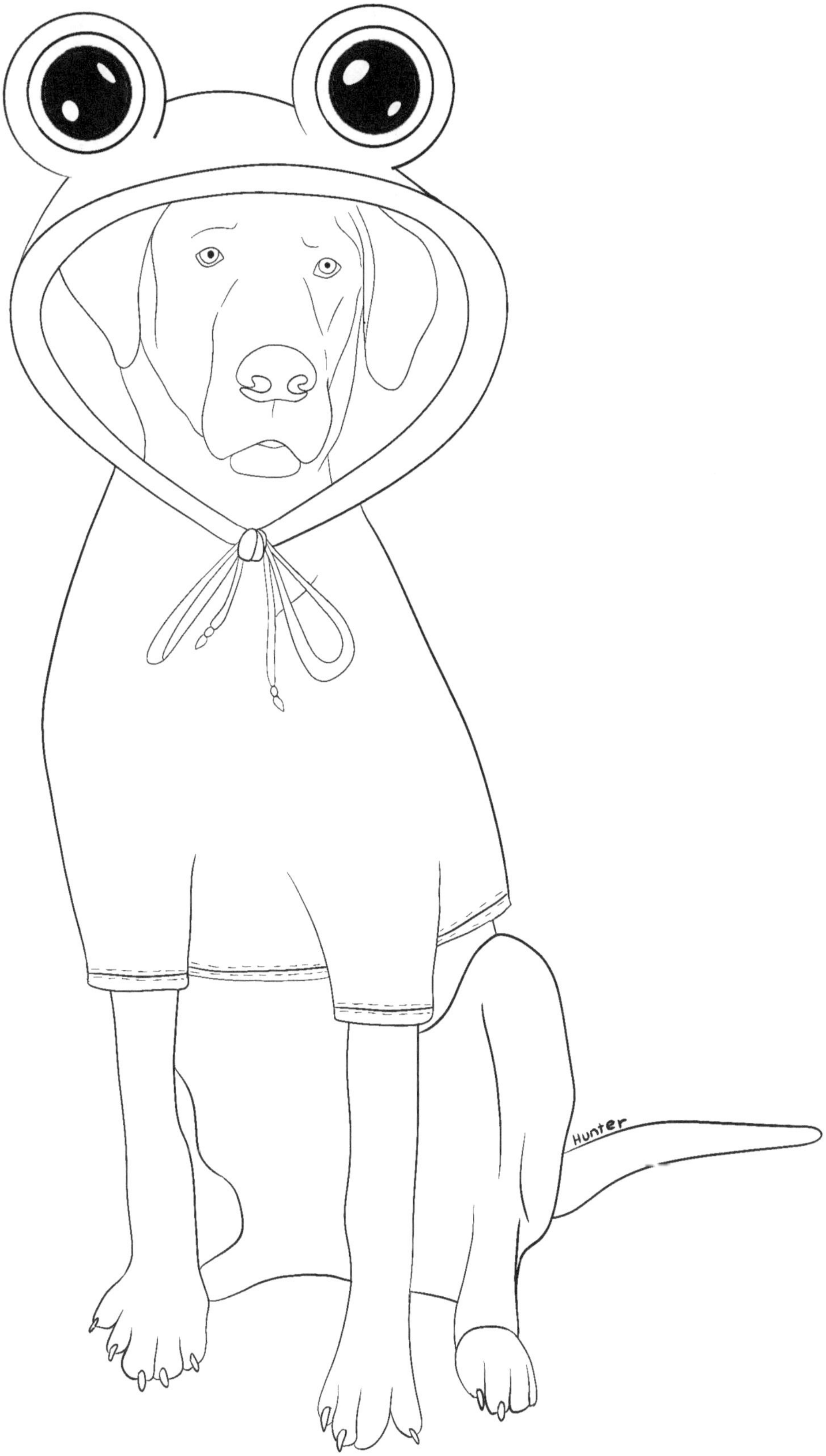
Hunter

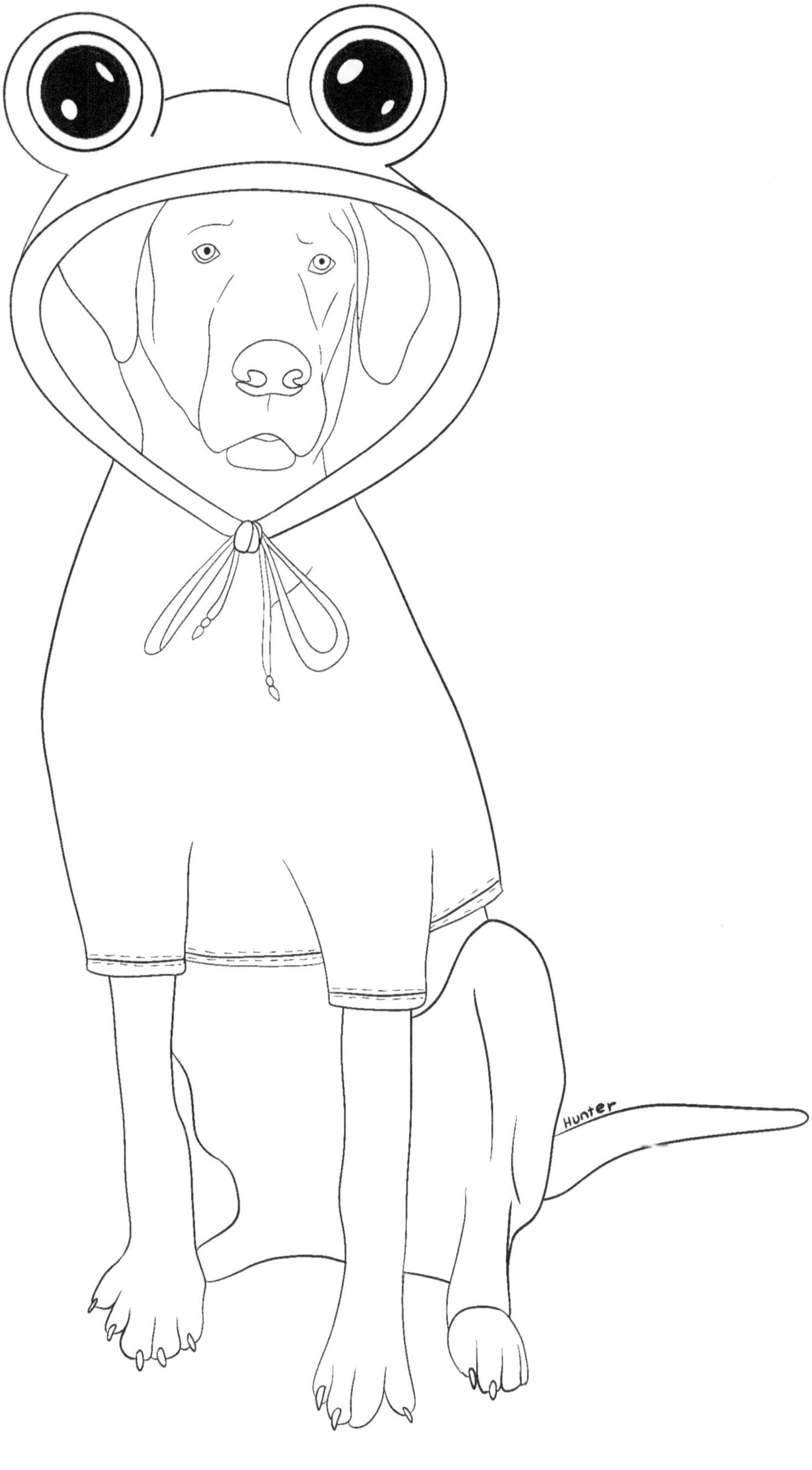
Hunter

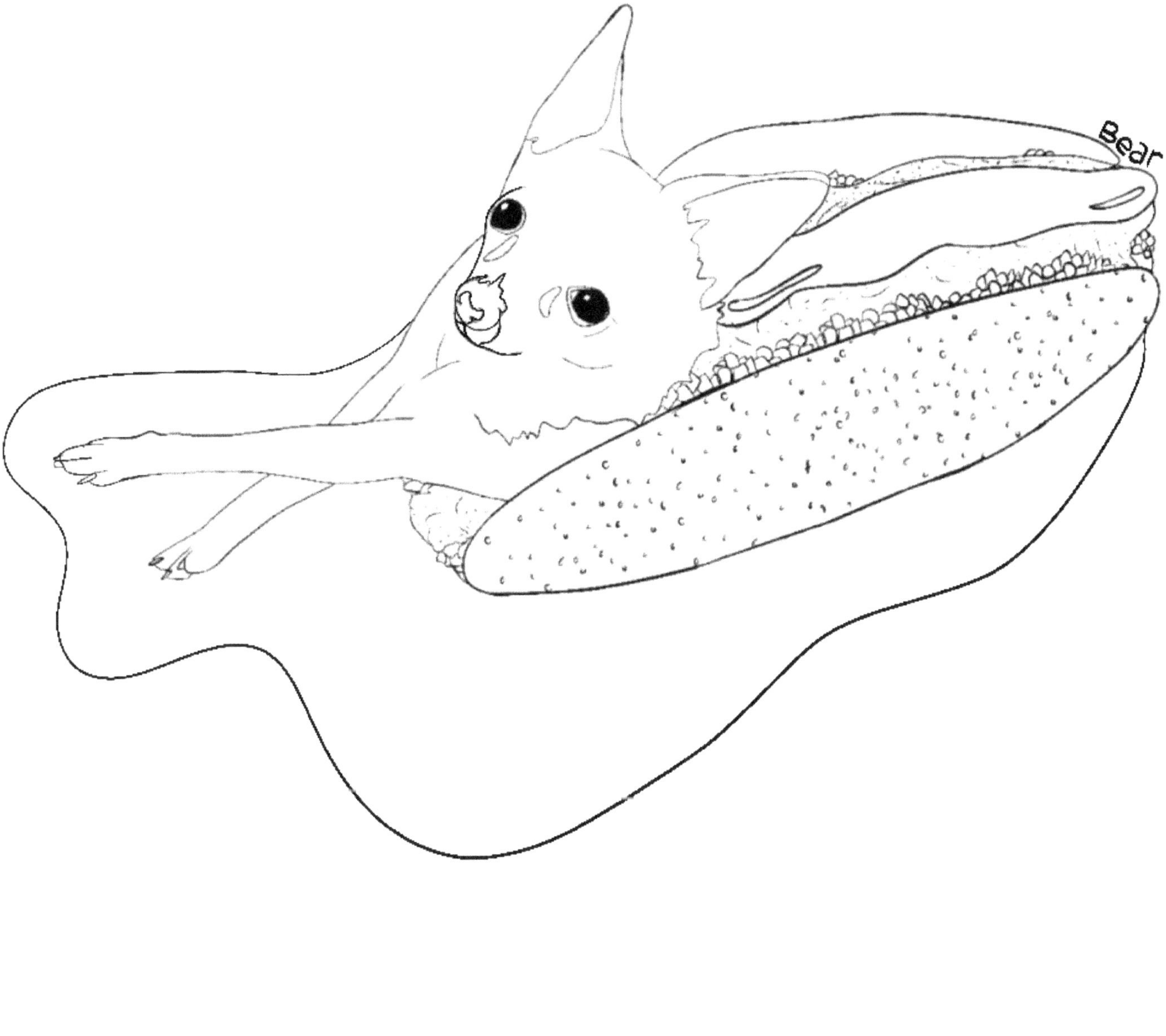
Bear

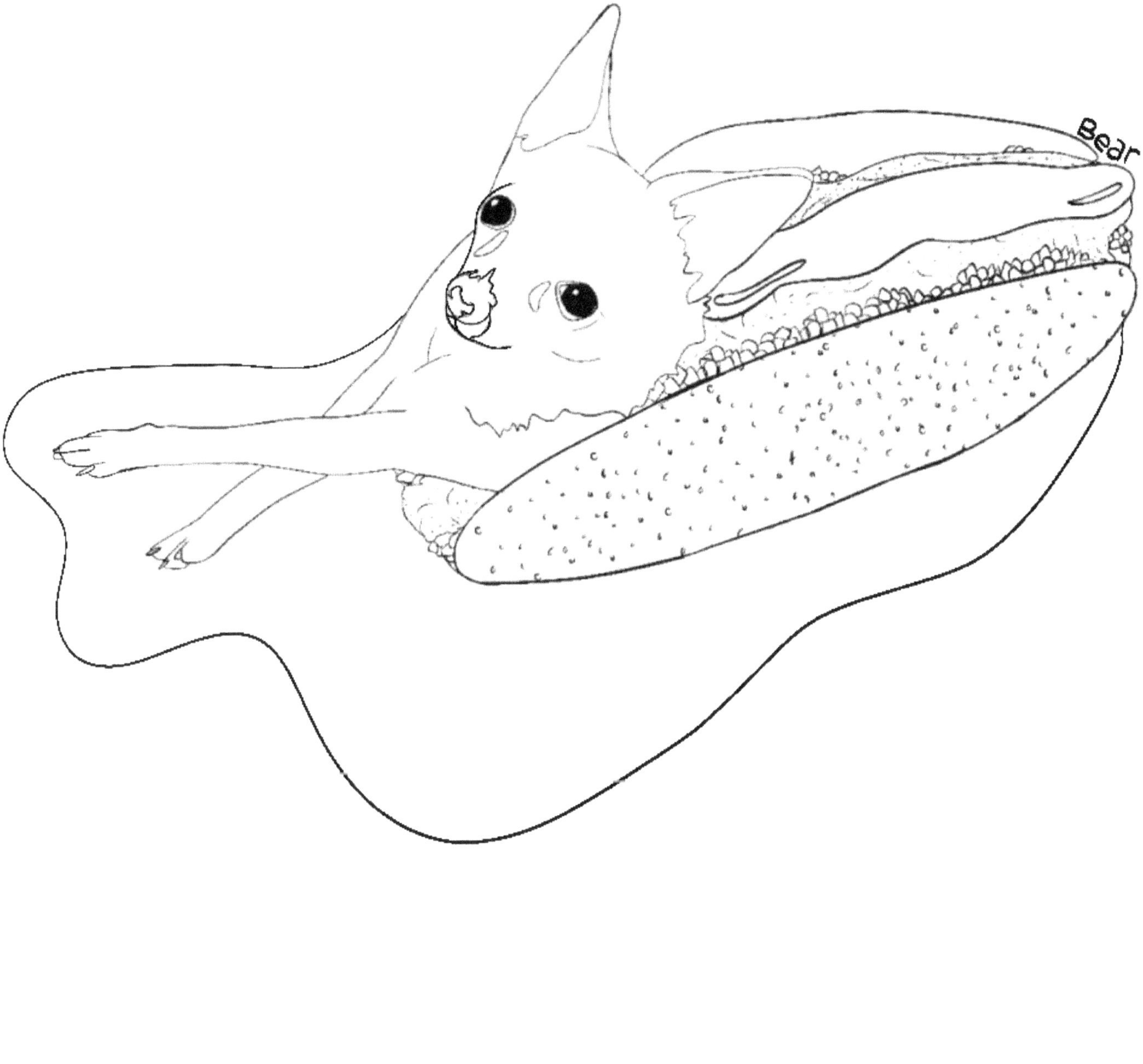
Bear

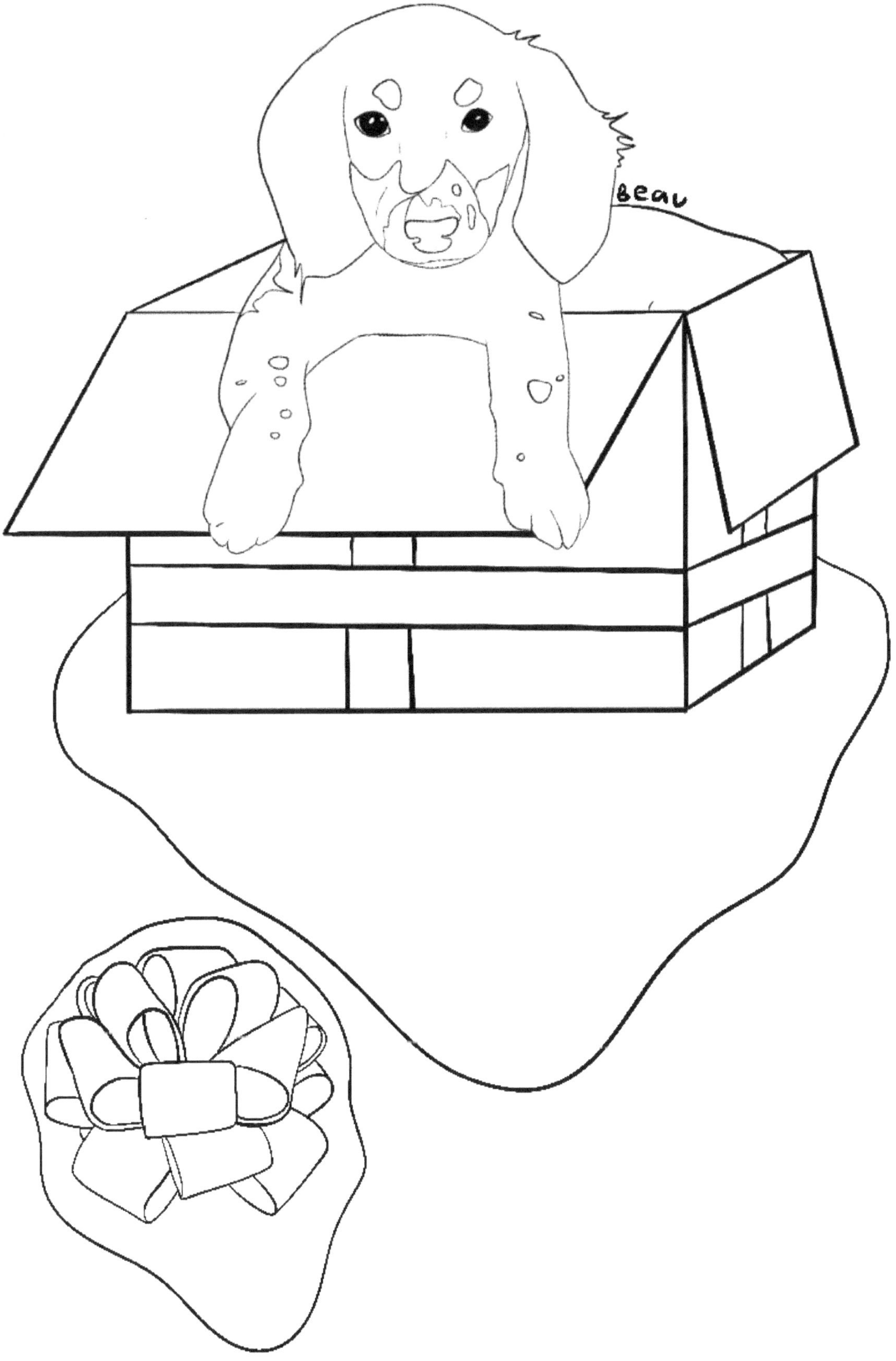
BEAU

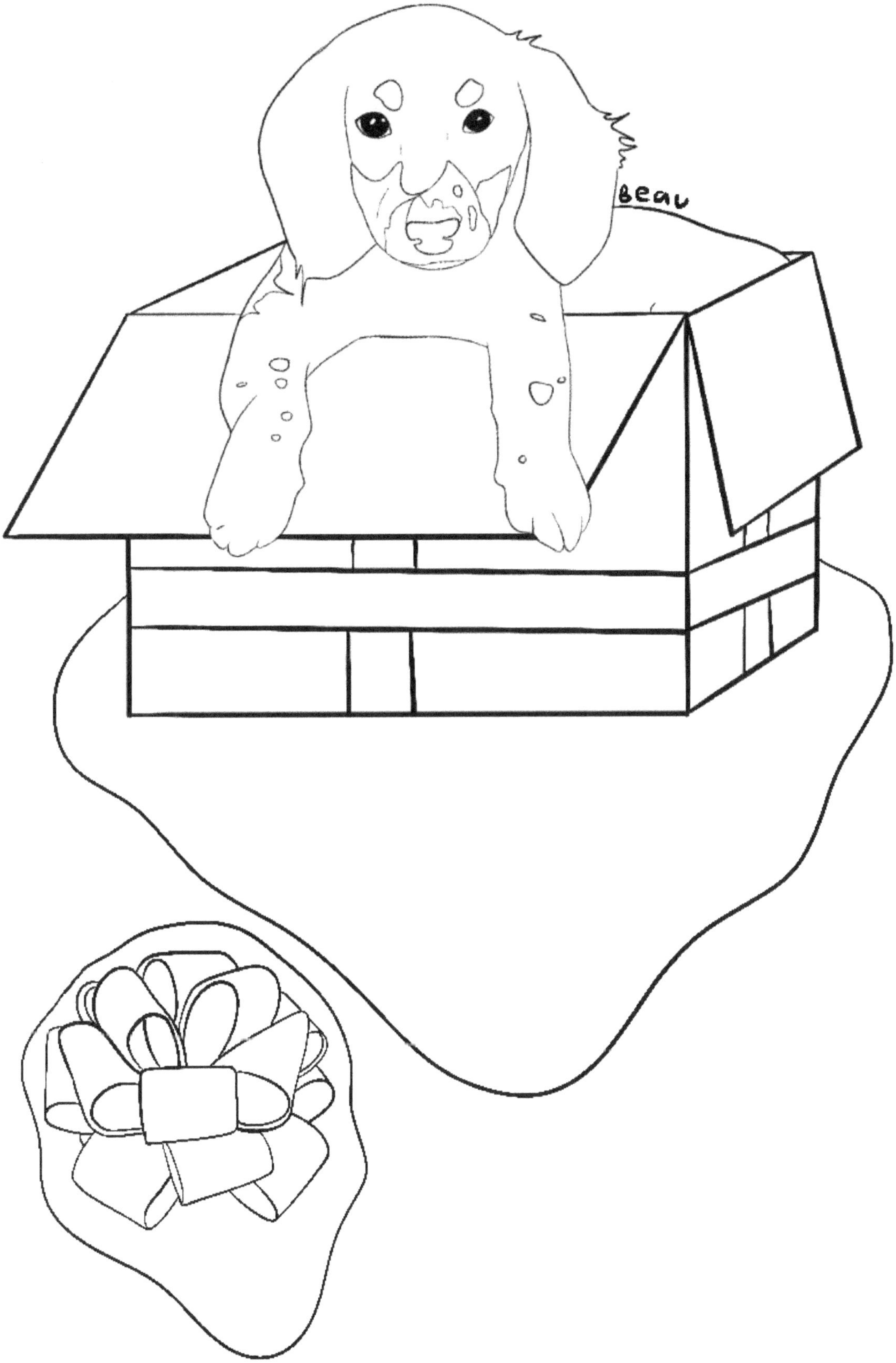
Beau

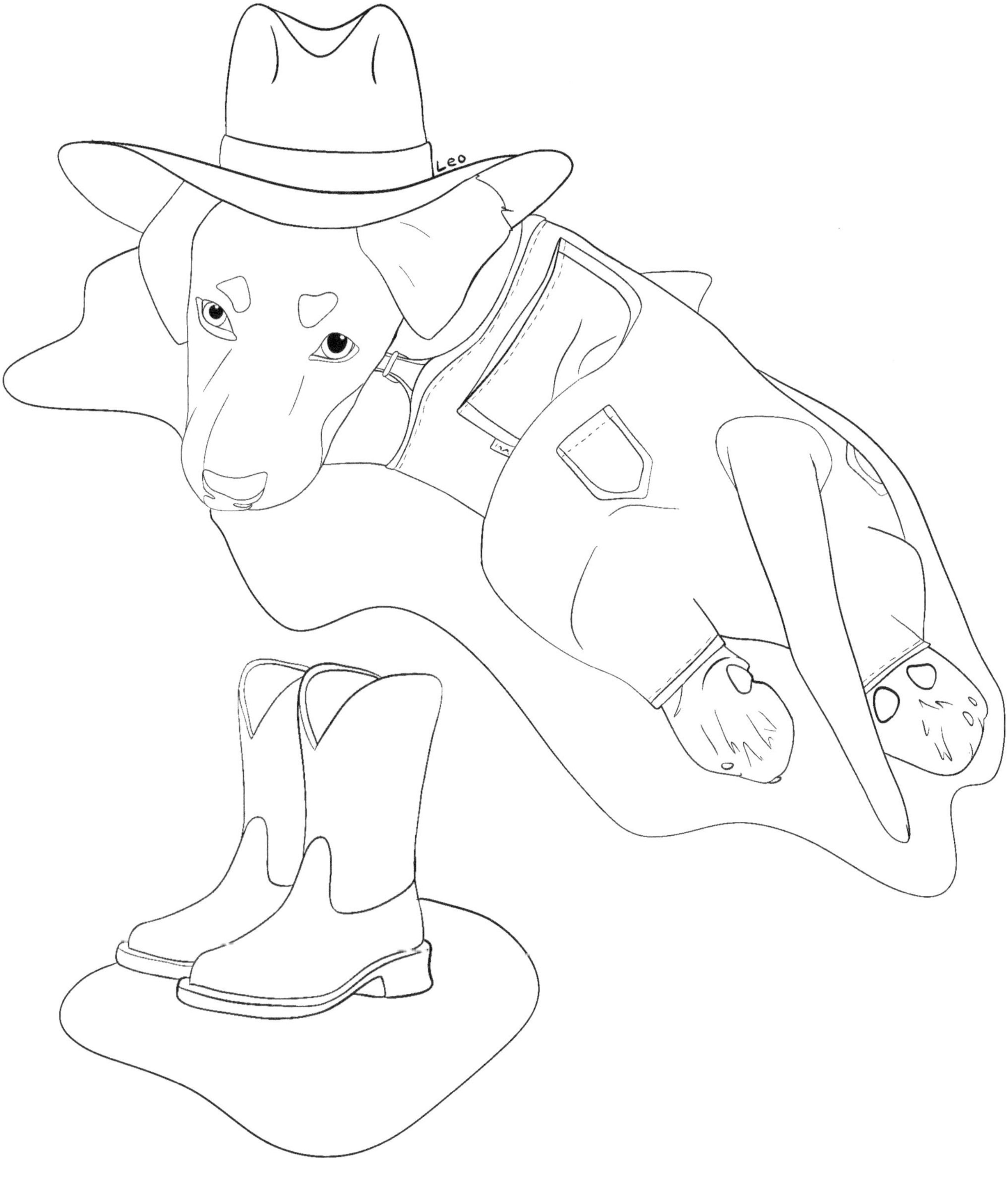
Leo

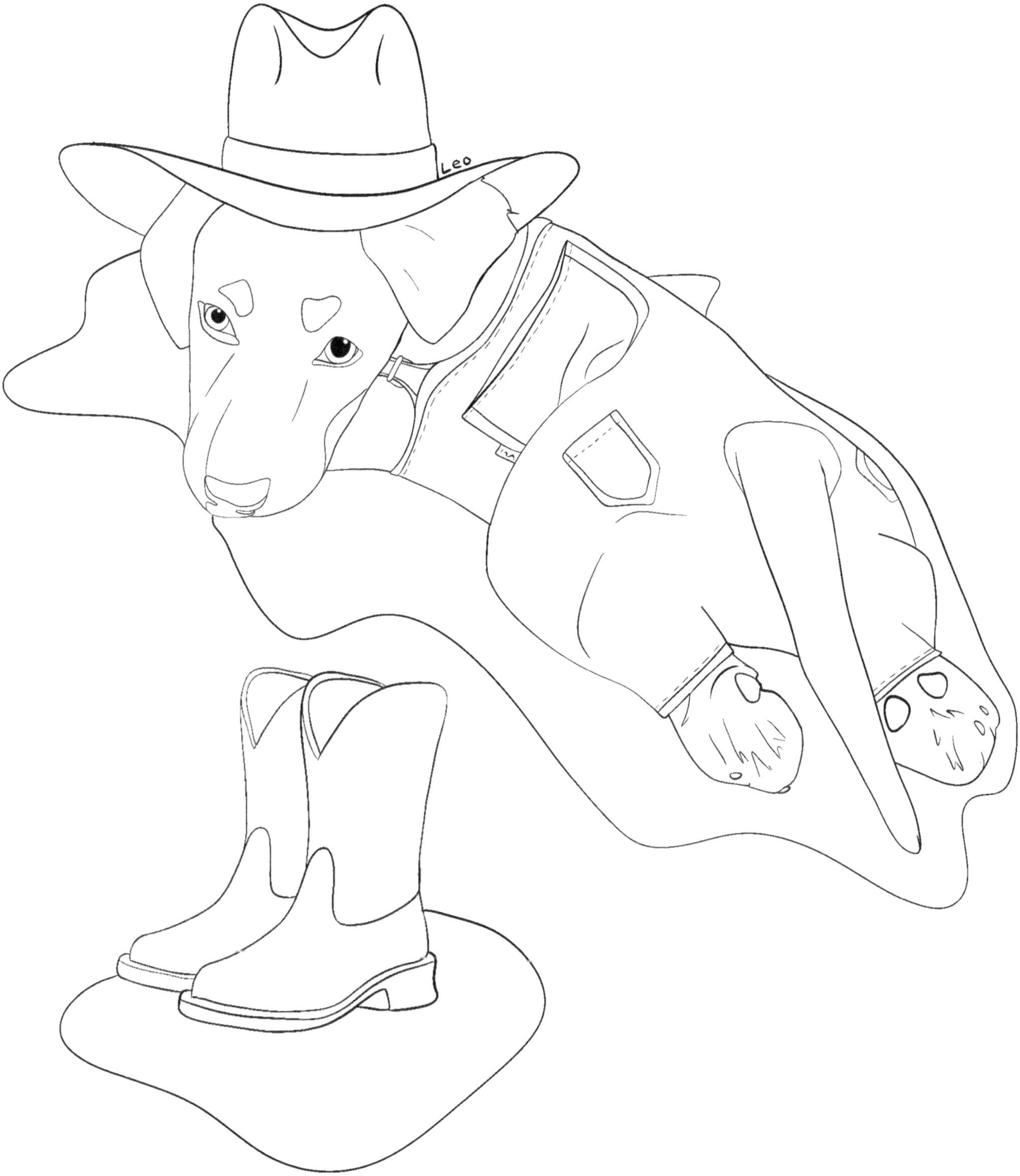
Leo

www.ingramcontent.com/pod-product-compliance
Lightning Source LLC
Chambersburg PA
CBHW081512220526
45467CB00010B/2892
* 9 7 9 8 3 8 7 7 4 3 9 2 4 *